HOW TO CHOOSE YOUR BABY'S LAST NAME: A HANDBOOK FOR NEW PARENTS

SIX CONVERSATIONS TO HAVE
BEFORE CHOOSING YOUR CHILD'S SURNAME

LORELEI VASHTI

Copyright © 2019 by Lorelei Vashti

All rights reserved.

All rights reserved. This book or any portion thereof may not be reproduced or used in any manner whatsoever without the express written consent of the author, except where permitted by law.

Cover design by Jess Cruickshank / The Jacky Winter Group

Second edition, updated 2019

ISBN: 9780648730408

www.loreleivashti.com

To Jeremy, for his love and support

CONTENTS

Acknowledgments	vii
Author's Note	ix
Introduction	xi

PART I
WHAT'S IN A NAME?

1. What meanings do last names hold?	5
2. What is your partner's opinion of their last names?	23
3. But what do last names actually represent?	31
4. Genealogy	43
5. Is it legal?	47
6. Cultural variations	51
7. Ch-ch-ch-ch-changes	55
8. Talking with your partner about last names	59

PART II
HELP! WE DON'T KNOW WHICH LAST NAME TO USE!

PART I
OPTION 1: FATHER'S LAST NAME

1. Issues to consider with this option	81
2. Discussing this option with your partner	87
3. Difficulties (or lack of) resulting from this choice	97
4. Regrets (or lack of) arising from this choice	107

PART II
OPTION 2: MOTHER'S LAST NAME

5. Issues to consider with this option	119
6. Discussing this option with your partner	127

7. Difficulties (or lack of) resulting from this choice — 133
8. Regrets (or lack of) arising from this choice — 137

PART III
OPTION 3: HYPHENATED OR UNHYPHENATED DOUBLE-BARRELED LAST NAME

9. Issues to consider with this option — 147
10. Discussing this option with your partner — 153
11. Difficulties (or lack of) resulting from this choice — 161
12. Regrets (or lack of) arising from this choice — 167

PART IV
OPTION 4: A BLEND OF BOTH

13. Issues to consider with this option — 171
14. Discussing this option with your partner — 175
15. Difficulties (or lack of) resulting from this choice — 179
16. Regrets (or lack of) resulting from this choice — 181

PART V
OPTION 5: ALTERNATING LAST NAMES FOR SIBLINGS

17. Issues to consider with this option — 185
18. Discussing this option with your partner — 189
19. Difficulties (or lack of) resulting from this choice — 191
20. Regrets (or lack of) arising from this choice — 193

PART VI
OPTION 6: A NEW LAST NAME

21. Issues to consider with this option — 199
22. Discussing this option with your partner — 203
23. Difficulties (or lack of) resulting from this choice — 205
24. Regrets (or lack of) arising from this choice — 207

Other naming options to honor your families	209
Final words about last names	219
About the Author	239

ACKNOWLEDGMENTS

An enormous thank you to Jeremy Wortsman, Nikki Lusk, Sofija Stefanovic, Geoff Waite and Ian Rogers for publishing and editorial support.

And a special thank you to everyone who took part in the survey, and shared your naming stories—this book wouldn't exist without you.

AUTHOR'S NOTE

Some names in this book have been changed for privacy reasons.

INTRODUCTION

If you're reading this book, you're probably in the midst of a baby last name dilemma. Whether the arrival of your baby is imminent, or far off in the future, something has made you start considering your baby's last name now.

This book is here to help you think through the different options and, more importantly, to help you start *talking* about it with your partner.

The burden of choice

These days, you have choices about which last name your baby ends up with, and that's a wonderful thing. But it's also a difficult thing!

Choices are great, but when we have lots of them (father's last name, mother's last name, hyphenated last names, blended last names, alternating surnames for siblings, a completely new last name!) it's easy to feel paralyzed. In some ways it was easier when there wasn't a choice—babies simply inherited their dads' last names and that was that.

But times have changed, and for many families these days, automatically passing on the father's last name doesn't always seem right. With so many women retaining their birth names after marriage, and family identities changing, it makes sense for many people to reconsider their children's last names too.

Each family is different, and that's why, despite the difficulty, it's worth making your child's last name a decision that suits your own individual family, rather than just a default.

A very modern dilemma

Since medieval times, the majority of couples in the West—including the United States, United Kingdom and Australia—have passed on the father's last name to the baby. While there have always been instances and exceptions to this rule, it remains a dominant social convention.

However, with the fight for equal gender rights, many of our social conventions have changed too. We're now living at a time when it's much more common for married women to keep their own name; when same-sex marriage is becoming enshrined in legislation in more places around the world; and when many couples don't marry before having kids. Of couples that do marry, those in both heterosexual and same-sex relationships often choose to retain separate last names. As a result there are now more and more couples who embark on the joyful pursuit of building their family starting with two different last names.

It's a very modern dilemma!

A decision, not a default

Last name choices are changing because families are changing. Many of us grew up with mothers who kept their last name after they married, or in blended families where family members had different last names. We may have changed our last name to a stepfather's name, or gone back to a mother's maiden name when we were teenagers. Whichever way you look at it, the idea of the traditional nuclear family is changing. Nevertheless, the practice of passing on the father's last name has remained.

But many people aren't aware that your baby's last name does not just happen by default or accident—it can be an active decision that parents make together. In the United States, United Kingdom and Australia, there is no law that says children must only take their father's last name.

Many couples are happy to continue the tradition and pass on the father's last name. But for others, that tradition has become increasingly jarring and uncomfortable. Over the past few decades, many families have been searching for—and finding—alternatives.

No right answer

There is no right answer to the last name dilemma and, interestingly, people's perspectives on what they should do don't always fall along gender lines. Many women say they would prefer their children to inherit their male partner's last name, and there are men who won't allow their name to be passed on to their child, for personal, political or aesthetic reasons.

I think it's really helpful to hear lots of different individual's stories, which is why this book is full of them. I surveyed more than 150 people from the United States, United Kingdom and Australia, and asked them how they chose, or plan to choose their child's last name. Learning about their experiences will, I hope, remind you that you have choices, and that you'll need to make the one that's most right for you, as a family.

My story

This book wouldn't exist if I hadn't gone through this very dilemma. My partner Jeremy and I started discussing our daughter's last name during my pregnancy.

His last name is Wortsman, mine is Waite (although I use my middle name, Vashti, as a pen name). We're not married, and even if we were, we'd both have kept our own last names. We didn't want to hyphenate our last names because we felt it would be too clunky, so we needed to choose one or the other: Waite or Wortsman.

But neither felt entirely right to us; neither felt entirely fair.

During this time I reflected on how, for many people, last names aren't really that significant; lots of my friends didn't understand what the big fuss was. Why agonize over something so trivial? Why not just go with the easiest solution—Jeremy's last name—and forget about it? But for us, the decision wasn't straightforward, because we felt the last name mattered as an expression of our daughter's identity.

Jeremy and I tried to figure out what the best solution for us might look like. We sat up late in bed on our phones, synchronized googling, trying to find out how other families had solved this problem, but we couldn't find much information to help us. Strangely, it was difficult to even find out what the law in our state said about last names, so we were confused as to what options were even in our legal power.

It wasn't exactly an argument, because there didn't seem to be any right or wrong, but still we jumped back and forth testing out all the sides. Who was the most attached to their last name? Which last name held the most meaning? It reminded me of that river-crossing puzzle where the farmer has a fox, a goose, and a bag of beans, and he has to get them all to the other side of the river in a boat but can only take one thing at a time. If we gave her my last name, would Jeremy feel less of a connection to her? If we gave her Jeremy's last name, weren't we just going along with an outdated tradition that didn't reflect our values as a family? No matter how many different ways we tried to make it work, we could not get all our possessions safely to the other side.

I was more than halfway through my pregnancy and we still didn't have a last name for our daughter. "We're going to have to give her your name after all," I wailed to Jeremy, ready to give up and take the easy option out. I was dramatically unhappy. I felt defeated by everything: by history, by logistics, by our utopian vision of a fairer world.

Then, Jeremy brought up a last name option we had briefly joked about months earlier. We'd melded both our last names and started referring to our baby as Waitsman. At first I thought this sounded ridiculous: a tabloid-ready blend, akin to fusing the celebrity couple names Brad Pitt and Angelina Jolie into Brangelina (RIP). But as we flailed deeper and deeper in the mire of last name options, it started sounding less absurd.

When Jeremy told me he liked Waitsman, I felt a massive weight lifting off my shoulders. I actually had tears well up! This solution finally felt right. So we decided to give our daughter the last name Waitsman.

We still weren't sure if what we wanted to do was even legal. We wrote her name on the birth registration form and waited to see what would happen. Six weeks later, her birth certificate arrived in the mail, and there it was: Waitsman.

Why had it been so difficult to get to this point?

Why I wrote this book

This book came about because we couldn't find any resources on this topic when we were deliberating on our baby's last name. Despite living in a very socially progressive city, most of the parents we knew had passed the father's last name on to their children (even when the mother had a different last name). I wanted to reach out to those who had found alternative solutions, to talk to them and ask them about their decision-making process: how did they come to an agreement? What obstacles did they face? What advice did they have for others? And did they have any regrets? I now understood that this was a very personal issue, with many contributing factors. I thought it might be useful to gather interviews, and share how various people navigated the baby last name dilemma. Then couples facing the dilemma anew could consider a variety of options, and make the decision that works for their family.

So here it is: a book that clearly outlines all the options, so you can talk about them together and search for the one that feels most right for you and your family.

About me

I'm a writer and editor who has made a career of researching and writing about anything that captures my interest. From pop culture and vintage fashion, to birth and parenting, I've published in magazines, newspapers and literary journals. My first book, *Dress,*

Memory: A Memoir of My Twenties in Dresses, was published in 2014.

I don't have any professional qualifications in the area of social trends or genealogy, but I'm a parent with a passionate interest in names (both first and last)—in their history and their meaning, in their role as a signifier of social change, and in what they tell us about ourselves. I've been researching this topic for more than two years, and believe I'm the only person to offer a comprehensive guide in this field.

What's in this book

This guide gives you all the relevant information in one place, to help you make the decision that works for your family. While I firmly believe every couple needs to make the decision for themselves, I hope to demonstrate that it's currently more acceptable than it's ever been to make a non-traditional last name choice—and every year it becomes more and more "normal".

By giving you an insight into other couples' decisions, this book will expand and open up the conversation you can have with your partner and even your extended family. It's written for women and men, straight couples and same-sex couples, couples that are more traditional and couples who would willingly describe themselves as flamboyant. I'm confident that, whoever you are, somewhere in this book is the answer to your baby last name dilemma.

The anecdotes that came through the survey results are

eye-opening. People in their fifties reflect on the decision they made decades ago, and people who have just reached their twenties, who aren't close to having kids yet, ruminate on what they might do in the future. There are couples who have had to consider cross-cultural issues when naming their children, same-sex couples, couples now separated, and single and solo parents.

I hope that the stories you find here will help kick-start conversations not only with your friends and your family, but, most especially, with your partner. What better way to start your journey together as parents than by talking about the values that matter most to you? And these values will emerge, sometimes in a surprising way, when you start discussing the meaningfulness of last names with them.

Women have grown up feeling like their name is something they will be expected to discard. That may explain why there are more female than male voices in this book—when I did a callout on Twitter and Facebook for survey respondents more women than men seemed to have considered this issue more deeply. But lots of men had also pondered this issue, and I've found their insights thoughtful and valuable.

Fairness

One theme that underlines this last name issue is, of course, feminism. Despite what Men's Rights Activists might think, feminism is not about usurping men or trying to make them feel less "manly", nor is it about taking away paternal rights. It encompasses many things, but in a very basic way it's about gender equality. Many people feel strongly that women's names and histories have been lost over centuries because of this male-last-name tradition, and that, by keeping it going, we're favoring men.

If you're uncomfortable with the word "feminism" you could also just call equality by its old playground name: fairness. If you consider your heterosexual relationship to be an equal one, and that you are a team or a partnership working together, then the fair thing to do is to discuss each other's preferences for your baby's last name, rather than assuming it will automatically be one thing or the other. For some couples this conversation might take nine seconds; for others it might take nine months.

For everyone, at some stage, it will probably get emotional.

Some statistics

According to an analysis by the *New York Times' The Upshot* blog in 2015, about 30 per cent of heterosexual women in the United States in recent times decided to keep their birth names in some way after getting married. (Around 20 per cent retained their birth name in full, and another 10 per cent opted to hyphenate their own last name with their husband's name.) This is an increase since the 1980s and 1990s, when only 14 per cent and 18 per cent of women kept their birth names respectively.

In Britain, the trend for married women taking their husband's name seems to be going down in recent years too: In 1994, 94 per cent of women took their husband's last name; academic Rachel Thwaites found that this had gone down to 75 per cent in 2013.

In Australia, the figure is estimated to be around 80 per cent of married women who assume their husband's names upon marriage.

With these numbers shrinking, as well as an increase in couples having children in common-law or de facto relationships, the amount of couples who begin their parenting journey with two different last names has also increased, so the question of whose last name any children will get is becoming more and more relevant to society at large.

Recent findings on children's last names

In a study presented in 2012, Australian researchers Deborah Dempsey and Jo Lindsay found that approximately 90 per cent of Australian children in the state of Victoria have their father's last name (this figure doesn't include children who have hyphenated last names made up of both parents' names). This figure mirrors similar research done in the United States.

Using data from the Victorian Registry of Births, Deaths and Marriages from 2005 and 2010, Dempsey and Lindsay broke the statistics down further and discovered that 75 per cent of children with unmarried parents have their father's last name.

This figure particularly interested me, because the majority of my friends who have kids aren't married.

A conversation with Dr Deborah Dempsey, senior lecturer in sociology at Swinburne University of Technology in Melbourne, Australia

In late 2014, I spoke to Dr Dempsey, who, as part of the aforementioned study, surveyed almost a thousand participants about the last name choices they'd made for their children. It was such an interesting conversation, and opened my eyes on where our society seems to be on this issue.

Why do you think most children still get their father's last name, even when the mother hasn't changed her last name?

Some women said that they didn't think their partner would consider an alternative, and they hadn't actually discussed it. Some women seemed to be saying: I gave birth, so therefore it's okay for him to have something —it's a visible display of the fact that he's the father. Other women worried that it would be thought that the child's paternity was unknown. And some people talked about the expectations of extended family and wanting to recognize the paternal extended family, particularly in cases where the parents weren't married.

Did women talk about their reasons for giving the male last name?

A lot of women talked about the social ease of their decision: how it's going to affect extended family, and also how it's going to be received at [the child's] school. A lot of people talked about the school environment and not wanting their privacy breached or their family singled out for attention, if they did something that was against the norm. I think a lot of people probably wouldn't see themselves as conservative, but they really want to go under the radar. They don't want to make a decision that's going to draw attention to themselves in any way.

Do you think people know they have a choice?

I think people do know there's a choice, but [they] either decide that they like the convention, or it was just taken for granted that everyone would have the same name.

I think, particularly among unmarried parents, there is more discussion and negotiation about the last name issue, but they tend to resolve the issue in favor of the father's name.

For me it was simply about fairness, and for my partner too.

For the people who opted for the less conventional choices, that was really the central issue—for the women particularly. "It's only fair that my name is reflected because that's equal. That's a more equal way of organizing it." Some talked about more explicitly feminist views [but a lot of people] just talked about it being fair. "It's democratic, it's an egalitarian decision that we're making here".

But one thing that I do find really interesting is that solutions like yours, where you create a new name, were actually more popular than hyphenated names for married couples. But hyphenated names are a bit more popular for unmarried parents. So 7 per cent of children born to unmarried parents have hyphenated last names. And about 3 per cent of children born to unmarried parents have a newly created last name. You can't really explain that, but it's really interesting.

What is the purpose of last names these days?

The first thing that came into my head is that last names indicate belonging. What we've also been using in our work is this idea of "display", which comes from the work of a British sociologist called Janet Finch. It's just this idea that names actually *do* something. They're not just private, they're public. And they announce to a public beyond the family who this child is, and what their place is. But privately [last names] are a very powerful symbol of belonging to the people who give them, use them, and claim them.

Do most people recognize that children can have a different name to their parents?

There are so many stepfamilies and blended families, but I think names are still a powerful symbol of family unity. Some people are really happy to play around with [names], but a lot of people have this really strong sense that the name marks us out as a family unit. And in this day and age, 75 per cent of married parents and [their] children all have the same name as each other. It's a dominant convention that the name says who you belong to, and that "this is our unit". I think people still worry about being different!

A lot of people like to do what's perceived as normal. But then again there's lots of examples of people doing things like you and your partner have done. Some of the innovations that same-sex couples come up with get adopted and incorporated into unconventional heterosexual couples' decision-making.

What sort of people are more likely to make an unconventional choice?

[People who are all] about creating something that's looking to the future. Not everyone wants to have the continuation of the male line and the continuation of patrilineage.

A lot of people say: "What about your children, what are they going to do in the future when they've got a hyphenated or unhyphenated double-barrelled name?" The people who are comfortable with that decision tend to say: "Well they'll just decide how they want to handle it, it's up to them."

The other thing is: traditions are reinvented all the time. Traditions that we often think of as really ancient are actually quite modern. We've only had last names since [around] the eighteenth century. Some people are happy to play around with traditions, and others won't.

I think it's fair to say that there's a lot of power attached to naming someone. So it was interesting to us that more women weren't asserting their right to use their name. There's still evidence that a lot of men are quite invested in the idea of their children having their name.

It's a very emotional topic. I shocked myself with how upset I was getting over it!

The interviews I did for this project were probably the most enjoyable of any I've ever done for my entire career! Because people love talking about this topic, it means a lot to them, particularly to women. Men aren't particularly interested in it, because they're in a position of privilege with regard to this issue, so it's just not something that's particularly on their radar. We had trouble getting men to take part.

Does your research tell you which last name choice is 'better' than all the others?

There's no better choice [of last name] than any others. But at the same time I think [it's part of a bigger context]—we know that married relationships are still not equal, that there are a lot of deeply entrenched gendered inequalities that only come out at the point of marriage. Particularly when people have children, divisions of labor between men and women become much more distinctive and based on gender lines.

I think the point [Lindsay and I] are making in [our research] paper is that: if this really were a level playing field, we'd see much more evidence of mothers [giving children their] names. We're seeing a bit of tinkering around the edges with a patriarchal and a patrilineal convention, but not much. You can look at surnaming as a case study of gender inequality in some ways.

I often talk to people who just have not ever thought about it.

They think it's trivial. Like housework is trivial. But actually who *does* the housework isn't trivial, you know?

I have trouble talking about this topic to my friends. It's really sensitive and personal.

Educated women are very sensitive about it. Because they don't like to see themselves as making conventional choices. Or making unfeminist choices.

A lot of people think that making an unconventional choice creates complications, and that you are always hassled and asked questions when dealing with bureaucracy.

That's not actually true. All it means is if you don't want to [be asked] awkward questions, you take along your children's birth certificate. And then there's no problem at all.

I remember speaking to a woman whose children didn't have their biological father's name, they had her name, and she was constantly being met with the assumption that he wasn't the children's father. And she said, "Look it's a pain, it doesn't particularly bother me, but it is kind of irritating." Because people just assume.

So it ultimately comes down to: what sort of person are you? Are you the sort of person who really worries about what other people think, or do you feel confident in your choices? Some people don't really care, and they're quite happy to stand out. And others are deeply uncomfortable with it.

A note about language usage in this book

This book is intended for everyone. Women and men, married couples, common-law couples, same-sex couples, trans and gender-diverse people, parents who share parenting with more than one person, single parents, parents who aren't in a relationship with the other parent of their child, and parents who are in a new relationship with someone who isn't their child's biological parent. I also recognize that, increasingly, many families are choosing to raise their children in a gender-neutral way. While it's complicated to address every family permutation individually, I've been mindful of the immense variation in personal circumstance when writing this book, and I hope that somewhere in the range and diversity of first-person accounts you read here, you'll recognize your own circumstances.

I've tried to gather true-life stories from a broad spectrum of people who live in the United States, United Kingdom and Australia. But it's impossible to encapsulate every person's individual family situation in a short book such as this.

A quick note about birth or 'maiden' names

This book doesn't go into the topic of women discarding or keeping their maiden names upon marriage. Some of the first-person anecdotes you read may touch on it, but to cover it in any depth here would distract from the issue at hand—which is what should you do when both parents *already* have different last names.

A postscript

I still get a shiver, two years later, when mail with my daughter's name on it arrives to the house. I love seeing her name. It makes me smile and it makes me happy; our solution feels right for us. Whatever last name you choose for your child, I hope it gives you this same feeling of rightness.

I
WHAT'S IN A NAME?

When choosing a last name for your child, there are a variety of opinions and approaches. That's why I like to think of this not as a book of answers but, rather, a book of questions.

Let's start with a really basic one.

What are last names, anyway?

In the West, last names are one of the ways we identify ourselves to other people. They are also a legal requirement.

In medieval Europe, where many modern Western surnames can be traced back to, people lived in small villages and were separated from other villages by large expanses of land. This distance meant that people from different villages didn't interact with each other much, and because everyone knew everyone else in the village there wasn't any need to have last names. People were known as John, or Catherine, or Robert, or Mary.

But as the villages and populations grew and people travelled more, there became a need to distinguish between those who had the same first name, and that's where last names came in.

But how do you make up a name out of thin air? The early last names came about in different ways, and were generally sourced from one of these four categories:

- patronymic last names—inherited from the father, so Adam's son would be called "Adamson"
- locative last names—a place name describing where the person was from; for example, "Boyce" comes from the French word *bois*, meaning wood, so it was a name for someone who originally lived in the woods
- occupational or status last names—such as "Clark", meaning a cleric or a scribe
- nicknames—"Dunn" means "dark" or "brown", and referred to hair color or complexion

By the seventeenth century, most people in Europe had started adopting last names, rather than just using a first name. As time went on, the last names became more and more diverse and complex, and today, as everyone knows, there are hundreds of thousands in regular use, as well as others that are constantly being introduced around the world.

1

WHAT MEANINGS DO LAST NAMES HOLD?

In our modern society, last names are primarily for formal identification. But of course, for many people, they are a lot more meaningful than this. Last names link us to a portion of our past. They sort people into family groups and clans, and can express unity, history, and pride.

We all have a different relationship to the last name we were given at birth, as well as any others we've added or discarded along the way. Whether you're a man or woman, straight or gay, your last name has a personal meaning that is unique to you, and these feelings will affect your decision about whether you want to pass it down to your children or not.

Not everyone loves their last name. Not everyone hates their last name. Some people find their last name incredibly meaningful. And many feel ambivalent towards it.

I love my last name

I love my last name. It's a Maltese name, which my 93-year-old grandmother already owned before meeting my grandfather who was also a Fenech—no, they were not related! I feel that it is such a big part of me; I could not imagine giving it up if I married my partner.

—Mary-Jane Fenech, mother of Iris Fenech-Smith

I like it; there's not many of us!

—Grace Imrie, mother of Lincoln and Eva Stephenson

I really like my last name because it's unusual and positive, but mainly because it just feels like it's very much a part of me.

—Jane Winning, mother of Elva Ribush-Winning

I love *my last name. Apparently it's from an orphanage in Italy called the Hospital of the Innocents. All the children were named Innocent who grew up there ... well that's what I heard and I'm sticking with it. Most people think I made it up and most other people just like saying "... and are you?" Our family don't talk about it much, it's our name and we're used to it, but I know we all secretly love it.*

—Andrea Innocent, mother of Luc Jacobs

I have great pride in my last name. It reflects my Yolngu (Indigenous Australian) heritage and lineage. It identifies my Clan Group and Traditional Land Ownership. It contextualizes who I am in the cosmos. For Yolngu people of Arnhem Land, last names are the marker of identity.

—Mayatili Marika, mother of Thomas and Tessa Griffin

I love the last name McGuire because it immediately tells people about my Irish ancestry, which I have on both sides of the family.

—Tim McGuire, single

Berrington is my married name, the only one in Melbourne. My maiden name was White and there are millions of them. I like my husband's last name.

—Patricia Berrington, married

I like my last name, and I'm the last in my father's family (in Australia) to have it, but I'd have been equally happy to have been given my mother's last name.

—David Laurence, in a relationship

It's my married name. I love the representation that it connects me to my husband and his family name. I wasn't going to change it, but with time I realized it meant a lot to me.

—Tanya Greenbank, mother of Andrew, Samara and Morgan Golding, and Shiloh and Saige Greenbank.

I love my last name. Hated my father. He died last year. I didn't go to his funeral and had not spoken to him for twenty years before. My last name is my *last name. Not his.*

—Catherine Deveny, mother of Dom, Hugo and Charlie Deveny-Borg

I hate my last name

I hate my current last name and have been embarrassed by it my whole life.

—Renae Whale, mother of Avery Carolan

Don't really like it, it's kind of a pain. But it's mine and I would never change it if I married (I don't understand that practice at all).

—Natalie Birdsley, mother of Christopher and Hazel O'Connor

My last name is from my ex-stepfather. My mother took on his last name when they married, and she had my and my brother's names legally changed from our birth surname. They got divorced in my early twenties, and it was nasty. I really hate my last name now and the only reason I haven't changed it so far is because my mother and brother still have it and I am not married to take on a different name. I would change it to my partner's, but we haven't had that discussion.

—Melissa Carter, mother of Finlay Inglis

Don't like it, it's my stepdad's name.

—Jo Turner, mother of Toby, Phoebe and Max Luce

I dislike my last name; however, I will be graduating into a profession and registered to a profession with it, so am likely to keep it down the line due to the professional connection.

—Lauren Collins, single

My relationship with my last name is complicated, but mostly negative. I don't have contact with my father's family, and have a distant relationship with my father. My mother changed her last name after they separated.

—Joel Turner, in a relationship

My last name is meaningful to me

My parents never had the same last name. I was given my dad's last name. But as both my parents have passed away I like having some part of his name.

—Rebecca Stock, mother of Logan Galea

I was given my father's last name at birth and chose to change to my mother's last name when I was sixteen because she raised me. I legally changed it at eighteen.

—Daine Singer, mother of Inez Singer

My father is Indian, and my last name is of Indian/Portuguese heritage. Although I'm half Indian, people usually assume I'm European, and so I find my ties to my last name valuable in my cultural identity. I also have a strong connection to my family.

—Sophie Fernandes, mother of "Roo" Fernandes

I am the last in my family to be born with it and there are no males to pass the name on ... this was disappointing to my dad who has a lot of pride in his Italian heritage, as passed on to him by his parents.

—Eva Ruggiero, mother of Harper and Ani Johnson

I'm a Hong Kong immigrant to the United States, one of a whole generation of women cousins with the last name Tam, with no male cousins with kids who are passing the name on. My children are Hapa (half Asian-Pacific-American) and I didn't know if they would look very Asian, very white, or very mixed—and I wanted them to have in their name something that was a cultural touchstone since I've left so much of my cultural heritage behind.

—Diane Tam, mother of Jude and Lou Tarricone-Tam

I like having the same name as my brother, sisters and cousins. I would be sad if either of my sisters changed their name. When we have family get-togethers we call them Megaparkerfest or Miniparkerfest depending on the number of participants. Sometimes we even print shirts.

—Megan Parker, mother of Iris O'Neill

I am quite close with my extended family, and our last name has some cultural significance to me and our greater family. It's a unique name and I am proud of it.

—Jason Scheltus, in a relationship

I took my wife's name when I got married. She is from a very close-knit family in Japan and I wanted this close family tie for my children. My parents divorced and my father passed away, so I don't have a close tie to my former family name.

—Mark Kaneko, father of Ayaka Kaneko

I'm the last in my line—I have only sisters and female cousins. It's not hugely a matter of pride, but it'd be a shame for it to disappear.

—Ben Birchall, father of Walter Birchall

It is my adoptive dad's last name and I'm very proud of it and its heritage. I chose to keep it when I got married as it is my identity and paid homage to my (not biological) dad.

—Lucinda Vainer, mother of Andrew Lake

As an artist, my last name is part of my identity, and it's also a connection to my father's side of my family. Coming from a family with a lot of women who've changed their names in marriage, I feel it's important to keep my last name and pass it along in some form to my children.

—Clare Rae, mother of Fox Palmerae

I was very close to my paternal grandfather and grandmother. I'm extremely proud of their contribution my family made during the Depression and Second World War to the Granville community.

—Anthony Fisk, father of Celeste Fisk

I like my last name, as it represents an important part of my identity. It's a Serbian last name, but I don't live there, so it's valuable to me as it signifies who I am and where I came from. I wouldn't change it.

—Sofija Stefanovic, in a relationship

I like my last name. I use it as a professional name so I'm attached to it in that way. Also that side of the family is more literary: they die early, get drunk more and have mental illnesses. Also, my dad died before I was born so I feel responsible somehow for the name.

—Laura Jean McKay, married

My name is a particularly difficult-to-pronounce Sinhalese last name, from Sri Lanka. It has sounds in it that are totally unfamiliar to the Australian English speaking mouth, and is really hard to explain how to pronounce. For that reason, I'm incredibly attached to it as a marker of my ethnic identity and as a daily reminder to people who want to classify me as "assimilated" or a "coconut" (brown on the outside, white on the inside) that actually I am Sri Lankan and they can't ignore that when dealing with me. I'm also a teacher, and think it's important that the students I teach have to learn to pronounce and respectfully engage with my difficult-to-pronounce last name.

—Sum Ambepitiya, married

My father was adopted by the Henry family. My mother was a Gerlach, but changed her last name to Cleal-Jones (Cleal is her mother's maiden name, Jones was her grandmother's maiden name) in her twenties. When my parents married, they both changed their name to Henry-Jones, to encompass both last names.

—Eliza-Jane Henry-Jones, married

It's rare and the heritage is a bit unclear. I feel bad because my mother kept her last name and she's the last person who'll have it. Because of my dad's parents they gave my brother and me dad's last name.

—Chris Dite, single

My last name is my grandfather's last name on my mother's side. I have my father's last name as a middle name, but my father isn't registered on my birth certificate because my mother didn't want him to be obliged to pay child support as I was an accident! My sister has her father's last name, which she always disliked as she wasn't close to him and his side of the family, and it meant she had a different last name to me and my mother.

—Zora Sanders, married

My last name is a large part of my identity. I am one of five kids and we are all incredibly close. We're a tribe and connect through our shared experience of growing up Lush.

—Amelia Lush, single

To be honest, I realize now I haven't given it much thought. Because I write, and have released books under that name, I imagine some people would say it's part of my "brand" (which is a concept that generally makes me gag). But I like it: "Law" sounds far more iconic and dignified than I'll ever be, and I think there was some sadness over the idea one of my sisters might surrender it when she got married. (She didn't, in the end.) I also like the story behind it: my Chinese paternal grandfather's family name was actually "Chow", but he bought a black-market birth certificate with the name "Law" on it so he could work in the United States. I like that there's criminal history to the name.

—Benjamin Law, in a relationship

My [last] name is my dad's first name, as is normal in Tamil culture. I like that it is Tamil because I'm proud of that heritage.

—Sushani Kandhan, married

No particularly strong attachment or cultural significance, but a sense that it is my father's heritage, and with no relations on his side of the family, no one else carrying on the family name, a sense that it is our only connection to his family and life before us.

—Luke Horton, in a relationship

I'm ambivalent towards my last name

I'm not particularly connected to the name itself, though it is what links me to my family, so of course that has some meaning.

I don't go around emblazoning my last name on the back of sweaters or anything though.

—Michelle Brown, mother of Aiesha and Alani Baiden

It is rare, but I'm not particularly attached to it.

—Lucy Filor, mother of Maggie Filor

It's more convenience and laziness that I haven't changed it [to my husband's name]. I like that it is a little unusual. I was adopted so would have had another name when I was born, although I don't know it.

—Louise Coulthard, mother of Alexander Fitzpatrick

I took my husband's last name. I don't dislike it, but almost four years on I still don't fully identify with it.

—Laura Rees, mother of Edward Rees

It's my last name. No real attachment beyond that. I used to hate it, but now I have accepted it.

—Lexington Heap, mother of Oliver and Lilith Sharp

I was born Pia Clements. My father was Robert Clements but he had been born Robert Cerveri. After the Second World War, when he was a primary school kid, his parents changed the family last name to Clements to protect, as they saw it, their three young children from post-war racism against Italian people. I was intrigued by this story and my Italian heritage from a young age, and when I was sixteen I unofficially changed my name to Cerveri, and did it officially at eighteen.

In some ways I love the name and its connection to my Italian heritage which I adore, but I've also come to have ambivalence about it due to the complexities of the character my father was and the relationship I had with him. When I had my children, I had a moment of considering giving them the name Clements rather than Cerveri to actually link them to my siblings, their extended family.

—Pia Cerveri, mother of Ori and Arlo Cerveri-Ward

It's just a name.

—Vu Ngoc Hiep Huynh, mother of Noah Huynh

I still have very mixed feelings about my last name. I have a complicated relationship to my father, so would have liked to drop his family name when I married, but didn't want to just take another man's name either.

—Lefa Singleton Norton, mother of Avery Singleton Norton

I have a confused relationship with my last name. When I was born my parents were not married and my father was about to leave on a Sea Shepherd campaign. My birth name was Dominic Iain (my father's first name) Francis (my mother's last name). My parents did stay together and later married at the request of my dying paternal grandfather. When they did, they both kept their birth names.

I registered for high-school with a hyphenated name (Banfield-Francis) and used this name until I was eighteen when I changed my full name to Dominic Banfield, dropping my middle name completely as I didn't want to have my father's whole name in my own. I did this for a number of reasons including a desire for simplicity and for my brothers and I to share the same last name, a mild preference for the name, and to allow the name to continue which it was unlikely to do otherwise. In hindsight I wish I had kept my birth name. This is because I am much closer to my maternal grandparents and have an enormous amount of respect and love for my mother. I didn't realize it at the time but because my brothers and I decided to keep Banfield instead of Francis, the Francis name is unlikely to continue as my mother only has sisters and they have all followed traditional patriarchal naming structures. I feel somewhat saddened by this, but I also do not place a great amount of importance in names so I don't see myself changing my name anytime soon. However, this confusion makes the idea of naming theoretical offspring even more complicated.

—Dominic Banfield, in a relationship

I feel so ambivalent about my last name. For one thing, there are so many Lucy Evanses in the world that in the early days of Facebook there was a Lucy Evans Society where all us LEs would chat. Most were lovely young women living in the United Kingdom, and a few actually started hanging out together. While that was a nice moment of Evans solidarity, for the most part I enjoy my first name, but find my last name pretty uninspiring.

Secondly, the etymology of Evans is "son of Evan". So I'm the daughter of Evans who's the great-great-great- etc. grandson of Evan. So many layers of male ownership.

Thirdly, I am estranged from my father. He's always been a problematic person in my life, and about six years ago I cut off contact completely. My mother didn't change her last name when she got married, and for a time I considered changing my last name to hers—Roberts. I didn't in the end because I wanted to continue to share my last name with my grandma (my father's mother). My mother's father (Ross Roberts) was himself a complex and not always positive figure, and my mother's mother (who I am very close to) remarried and now has the last name Skarratt. I concluded that I don't really have a strong connection to my mother's last name either, so there would be no point in tackling the administrative rigmarole of a name change. I also didn't want to have to answer difficult questions on public forums like Facebook, e.g. "OMG did you get married?" "No, just exorcising my deadshit father from my life" "...".

So my last name isn't something I take pride in, yet if I were to get married I would never want to change my last name. Maybe if my betrothed had a great last name to offer—Beveridge, Camelot, perhaps? But even then I couldn't. It always surprises me when women change their name when they marry. There's something so archaic about it. It speaks of ownership and one-sidedness.

A name is so tied up with identity as well. I couldn't imagine being anything other than Lucy Evans, and the good and bad associations that has for me. Maybe I kind of like that my battle scars are writ in my name. Taking on a new name would feel like whitewashing that history and identity.

—Lucy Evans, in a relationship

2

WHAT IS YOUR PARTNER'S OPINION OF THEIR LAST NAMES?

[He has] no real attachment to [his last name] other than it being an interesting name and one that has culturally recognizable connotations.

—Lee Sandwith, mother of Sailor and Rio Christmass

He is proud of his last name and his heritage. His grandparents were post–World War II immigrants and I think he's very proud of their achievements.

—Samone Bos, mother of Saffron and Jasper Bos

He likes it, I think. It's very important in Vietnamese culture, the last name. He has [even] more attachment to his middle name, which was made up by his grandfather and passed on to all the boys in his family. I think because he feels a sense of connection with his grandfather (now passed away) the middle name matters most to him. He was never determined for our child to have his last name, but if it had been a boy he very definitely wanted it to share the middle name.

—Kate Harris, mother of Georgette Nguyen

[She has] more attachment [to it] than I have to mine. Also a fairly rare last name, she is one of the last in her family to retain the name.

—Sam Scriba, father of Ari Scriba

He's white American, with Italian-American heritage on his father's side, and then white-mix on his mother's side. His Italian ancestry is important to him.

—Diane Tam, mother of Jude and Lou Tarricone-Tam

Definitely family pride around his last name—it's Russian and I think it makes him feel connected to that part of his family.

—Jane Winning, mother of Elva Ribush-Winning

My partner is so proud to be a Galea. He even has a tattoo of it on his arm. He feels like it represents his culture with his dad's side, who are Maltese.

—Rebecca Stock, mother of Logan Galea

I wouldn't want to answer for him but he has the kind of unvexed relationship to his name that most white middle-class men do. He didn't expect either his first wife or me to change our names (she did, I didn't) but neither did it occur to him to change his.

—Hilary Milton, mother of Clancy Milton Woolf

Scholz is quite a common German last name. My partner respects that the last name means a lot to his mother and father but personally does not feel tied to it. He also doesn't feel less connected to our son because they don't share the same last name.

—Elyse Truex, mother of Leon Truex

My partner has his mother's last name and identifies very strongly with his maternal extended family. His maternal grandmother is still alive, but the husband whose last name she passed on to her seven children died when the youngest was a baby. Three of her female children passed their last name on to the next generation so I would definitely describe the family as a matriarchy.

—Megan Parker, mother of Iris O'Neill

Pete has a mixed relationship with his name. He hates that he has to spell it out, "it's spelled like 'instead' but with a B in front" and he was teased about it as a kid with "garbage" puns. But, he grew into the name—all of his mates call him "Binny", some acquaintances don't even know his first name is Pete. His parents sometimes call him Binny too, and I'm guilty of it also. He has a brother who has married and his wife has changed her name to Binstead, so when/if they have kids there will be other Binsteads, but Pete was completely unwilling to consider that his child would not be a Binstead— even though he'll admit that it's just not a good name!

—Mary Masters, mother of Gideon Binstead

He is proud of his name. It was important that he share it with our children. He is the only son in his family so it was important to carry the name on.

—Carly Cook, mother of Charles, Louis and George Berghoferv

I think there is some pride and loyalty there. He isn't close with his family, but loves them very much and is immensely proud of the way he was raised.

—Darcy Laughlin, mother of Emily Milne

She loves her last name—it is cool and it is part of her identity.

—Ben Birchall, father of Walter Birchall

My husband has strong family ties to his last name and was disappointed when I chose not to change my name. His family are very proud of their last name.

—Lucinda Vainer, mother of Andrew Lake

I don't think she thinks about it that much. She wasn't very concerned about whether or not the children carried her last name as she was more focused on the relationship she would share with them rather than what names they would have.

—Pia Cerveri, mother of Ori and Arlo Cerveri-Ward

I think he mostly takes his name for granted and had never thought he would change it because it's not the conventional thing men do.

—Lefa Singleton Norton, mother of Avery Singleton Norton

Pride and connection to his father who died twenty years ago.

—Jo Turner, mother of Toby, Phoebe and Max Luce

He feels similarly to me about his last name. He likes it, and agrees that my last name is probably (marginally) a better/stronger name. He has emigrated to Australia from the United Kingdom so his attachment to his name has grown now that he is the only one (except for our daughter) from his family in this country.

—Ellen Angus, mother of Georgina Mant

He doesn't seem particularly attached. His parents are divorced and his mother kept her first husband's name, I guess so that she is still connected to her children. I always find that interesting.

—Andrea Innocent, mother of Luc Jacobs

I think he feels a connection to his family through his last name, it's part of his lineage and goes back many generations.

—Clare Rae, mother of Fox Palmerae

It has cultural meaning to him—a thing that connects him to Malta. He wasn't taught the language and has suffered racism. He has grown proud of his name and keeping it has felt like an act of subversion.

—Ada Conroy, mother of Pippa Conroy

My husband is a Junior and has a difficult relationship with his father, so has no great love for his last name. There were two branches of Sullivans in his small country hometown, and so there were several people with exactly the same name. It turns out my aunty by marriage was in the other clan and her brother was always getting calls intended for my father-in-law during their working life!

—Leah Emery, mother of Linka and Eartha Redzed

Joseph comes from a big Vietnamese family with a proud background. The Hoang family is well respected in the Perth Vietnamese community.

—Anthony Fisk, father of Celeste Fisk

3

BUT WHAT DO LAST NAMES ACTUALLY REPRESENT?

A big part of how we think about last names, and why we all have different responses to the question "What are they for?" is our own family background and the community we grew up in. If you felt an affinity to growing up as part of a tribe known as "The Brownings" then you might strongly identify with the use of a last name to create family unity.

If you've grown up in a blended family, brimming with new marriages and step-siblings or half-siblings, you might not have the same attachment to just one last name. You might have already changed your last name a few times, or seen your parents or siblings do it, and thus feel a connection to several different last names within your clan.

Once you open up a discussion about last names, whether it's in your close friendship circle, at a dinner party with complete strangers, or with your own partner, you will quickly see that different kinds of things are important to each person. Some of the central issues that stand out when discussing and deciding on a baby's last name are: identity, equality, family unity, the "sound" of it, connection, honoring family—or any combination of these things!

Last names can represent identity

I'd want my children to know where I came from. This is especially important to me, as my family doesn't live in that part of the world anymore (and Yugoslavia, as it was called when I was born – doesn't even exist anymore). I'd hate for that identity to be lost. I'd want my children to feel like they, personally, have a Serbian identity too.

—Sofija Stefanovic, in a relationship

[It is important for me to be] keeping my Tamil heritage and respecting the fact women do most of the work of making a baby.

—Sushani Kandhan, married

I don't want my children to have any connection with my father's family. Dad will be involved, but distant; his family will not be a part of our child's life. I feel no connection to the name, and would like to start fresh. If it weren't difficult and time-consuming, both my partner and I would change our last names to a wholly new name.

—Joel Turner, in a relationship

My partner is white, and I am brown. My greatest fear is that my child will be born with fair skin and no connection to their culture and no understanding of what it is to be a person of color. I want them to have my last name as a sort of extra Degree of Difficulty.

—Sum Ambepitiya, married

My last name has always played a huge role in my identity—it was a straight line to the people who mean the most to me. I know how lucky I am to be close to my family—especially my siblings who are all just freaking awesome human beings. All five of us have voiced our intention to keep our last name and to pass it on to our kids. I have to admit that I [find the idea of] the next generation in our family having Lush in their name really reassuring.

—Amelia Lush, single

Last names can represent equality

I want my children to know that their mother and father have absolutely equal standing in the family unit. That each family's history is equally important to them. That there is no more or less pressure on any child to "carry on the family name".

—Bri Lee, in a relationship

I like brevity, but I realize it may not be possible with a hyphenated name. Also do I want a child to sound like a law firm? But I don't like the presumption of patriarchy and being male or having male names as the standard, because it reaffirms sexism from the start.

—Angela May, single

It's vital to me that we don't simply give our children the father's last name, which is a tradition in our society that to me represents the time when wives were the property of their husbands. My husband and I came to our marriage as equals, so I'm interested in giving our children a name that doesn't favor one of us over the other, but that represents something important to both of us.

—Nikki Lusk, mother of Zoë Summers

[The last name should have] equal input from both partners, in recognition of the fact that we both would (ideally) contribute to parenting equally.

—Benjamin Law, in a relationship

It's important that we don't just blindly follow the status quo "just 'cause" and perpetuate societal expectations that limit our ability to accept change and make a better society for everyone.

—Lara Murray, in a relationship

Last names can represent feminism

For me, feminism and familial identity are more important than a strict "fairness" between parents, hence me wanting to give any children my name.

—Zora Sanders, married

It's about not carrying on sexist, patriarchal traditions that only value men/boys!

—Jessica Alice, in a relationship

Smashing the patriarchy? I'm super uncomfortable with patrilineal naming practices (as I am with wedding name changes) and would like at least some part of our own naming choices to push back against it.

—Luke Ryan, married

Last names can represent family unity

It is most important to me that all my children share their last name rather than the last name of both or one of their parents.

—Amelia Lush, single

I think that it's important for the whole family to share the same name—it helps build a collective identity. Other than that, I'm fairly flexible. Longer last names could potentially limit your choices for first names though, so if I had my heart set on a certain [first] name, I'd want to make sure it fit [with the last name]. I don't think the gender of either parent should really be a factor in the decision, and it's not really in mine, though I suspect my partner would be disappointed if I expressed a desire for our kids to have my last name.

—Brooke Sharpley, in a relationship

[The choice] depends on the child/person. Some people need to have a connection to their family as obvious as a name. I think it becomes increasingly confusing and isolating having different names to your family members (again, depending on the personality of the person) particularly if you have any kind of insecurities about your parentage/lineage.

—Susanne Hunter, married

Last names can be chosen for aesthetic or euphonic reasons

[When choosing a last name, it is important for me that my children] won't be teased as the result of any name they have. I would try to think of all the juvenile options for teasing. I wouldn't want the name to sound boring.

—Ledger McDavitt, in a relationship

[It is important for me that the first name] goes with the last name, I didn't want [a first name that is] too long, as our last name is. [It was also important to me] that initials or abbreviations couldn't be turned into names by bullies.

—Patricia Berrington, married

Length [is important to me]. I don't want my kid to be called McGuire-Van De Ven, for example. I'd rather just one or the other. But McGuire-Clarke would be okay. Also I want to avoid rhymes, so no McGuire-Perspire. In fact no Perspire, if I ever meet someone with that name.

—Tim McGuire, single

[It's important to me that my children] don't get lumped with something totally ridiculous and get tormented at school for it. A customer at work has the last name "Faggeter" and that is just so unfair on a kid.

—Chris Dite, single

I don't really care about family lines, so for me [choosing would be] based on what the last name sounds like, looks like, and means.

—Eileen Kenny, in a relationship

Last names can represent family connection

[I believe the last name serves as an acknowledgement] of the father—they may split from the mother and may not have a great connection with their child. I feel the name connection is important.

—Lauren Collins, single

If I had children I would want to share the same name as my partner and my child. My preference wouldn't be to keep my last name because a) I'm not that attached to it, b) I want to model a less patriarchal style of family structure and part of that is wrapped up in naming traditions, and c) I think it would be an adventure to take a new name.

—Alister McCulloch, in a relationship

I don't like the idea of my child having a different last name to me, as I'm not sure how easy it will be for us in terms of school documents etc. Also, would it help a child feel more connected to me as family (for example, if I adopt a child)?

—Daisy Brundell, single

Last names can be the result of many different considerations!

[My decision would be affected half by] politics, half trying not to burden the kid with a complicated name.

—Alex Maher, in a relationship

[My decision would be affected by] feminism, the aesthetics and sound of the name, the importance of the name, attachment to the name, the status of the name (whether it is common or rare).

—Ellie Higgins, in a relationship

[My decision would be influenced by] the views of my partner, first and foremost. Then, trying to predict how the child/children might identify with the last name. And then,

to a much, much smaller degree, the views of my parents/family.

—Sam Cooney, in a relationship

[My decision would be influenced by] feminism and family heritage, and trying to find a balance between these sometimes-competing concerns.

—David Laurence, in a relationship

[I would consider] the feelings of myself and my future partner (whether one of us particularly loves or hates their name and does or doesn't want to pass it on). [I believe the name should signal] the unity of the family group (sharing same or linked last names). [I would consider] meanings or connotations of the last name in our country/ies of residence or language/s of use. [I would consider how] well the children's full names flow together. [I would try to represent] the history/culture/heritage of our family.

-Jane Greenbank, single

I guess, as a gay man, there will be an extra parent involved in my kid's conception. It might be that my partner and I also need to consider our child's biological mother's wishes for the baby's last name, which means there would be three competing last names. I've always thought that whichever father to my child (i.e. my partner or myself) isn't biologically related to our child, we should use his last name, either by itself or first in a hyphenated combination. Someone passes on their genes, someone passes on their name. I think I like that.

—Tim McGuire, single

I've never believed in a wife taking the husband's name, so naturally the same issue extends to children. I don't really love *the alternating last names option, but the "making up a new one" option doesn't seem right to me either. Hyphenates are fine, but awkward. Honestly? None of them are good options to me, it's more about least worst.*

—Patrick Pittman, single

Most important is to have the decision made thoughtfully and collectively in conversation with my partner, and for it to represent both of us somehow. I also think it's important that the last name is not overly cumbersome, and will be convenient for our future human.

—Lucy Evans, in a relationship

It is important that both my partner and I are happy. I want to keep my name, and perhaps give one (or more) of my children my last name. But I respect his right to do the same. If we have one child they will take my name, if we have two they will have alternating last names. I doubt this will have any bearing on the children (to have different last names) given the shifting nature of families.

—Cassie Reynolds, in a relationship

The blended name won't work [for us], hyphenation is too long for those names, we have no attachment to another word that could represent us as a couple (though I like that idea) so we're stuck with either of our current last names. And I just feel like tradition would get to me. His and my parents would want it that way.

—Melinda Phelps, in a relationship

[A child's last name] should represent that they are a part of a family and that their parents are their father and their mother (or both parents [are fathers or mothers] in the case of same-sex relationships). It should also be a name that doesn't bring ridicule and is pragmatic—after all, children are cruel and there's no need to unnecessarily subject your children to bullying with a poorly chosen blended name.

—Andrew Webster, in a relationship

4

GENEALOGY

When Jeremy and I began discussing our last name options, I was really concerned about how future generations might trace our family lineage. I wasn't sure if making a less conventional decision would mess up our family tree forever. This anxiety became so acute that it made me want to disregard all my other concerns and opt for the easiest and most accepted option. I didn't want to feel the responsibility of having thrown part of our family history out the window.

So I spoke to genealogist Graeme Jaunay, who researches family lineage for a living, about what would happen to our records if we gave our daughter a last name that wasn't her father's.

He told me that, today, record keeping is significantly more detailed than it used to be, and the problem I was worried about is less of an issue than I thought. Birth certificates give parents' names in full—and a good genealogist starts with the subject and moves back in time, generation by generation, confirming all births with records.

He also reminded me that people have been changing their last names for many generations, so what we were proposing (giving a child a name that is not her father's) was actually nothing new.

Here are some situations where people may have made last name changes in the past:

1. a husband who adopts his wife's last name
2. stepchildren who adopt their stepfather's last name
3. an adopted child who takes the adoptive parents' last name
4. a foreign name altered to resemble an existing local last name
5. a male purchaser of property adopting the seller's last name
6. a misspelling at some point that is not corrected and becomes a new last name entirely
7. a name change as a condition for an inheritance
8. an admirer or lackey taking on a superior's name
9. someone hiding their identity for any number of reasons
10. a male rejecting his name for personal or societal reasons
11. a child taken/purchased/stolen from their natural parents

Jaunay adds: "As I tell my students: pursuing the origin of your last name may prove interesting, but the origin of your last name is *not* going to indicate the origin of your family!"

It's all food for thought when you're thinking about the real meaning behind your last name, its history and legacy.

5

IS IT LEGAL?

When Jeremy and I had our first baby in 2014, we didn't know whether or not it was even legal to give our child an entirely new last name. It seemed like it was *maybe* something people did, but we couldn't find anything written down that specifically gave us permission. And while we'd heard stories of other couples who had given their child a non-traditional last name, we didn't personally know anyone who'd done it.

In the end we decided to throw caution to the wind, and just write the last name we wanted on her birth registration form when she was born, and then wait for the authorities to write back and tell us that her name was unacceptable. They never did, which is how we found out we were allowed to do it.

I wonder how much the fear of doing something possibly illegal has stopped other couples from making a last name choice that might suit them better?

What the law says

The law in the United States, United Kingdom and Australia is that everyone must have a last name—they are required for identification purposes.

In the United Kingdom and Australia, you can give your child any last name you wish.

If you live in the United States, you will need to research your state's laws, as they do differ. While the legal universe of last names has opened up in recent years, and there is now much more flexibility than there used to be, there are still some states that insist parents can only choose last names for their children that are directly connected to their own, so be sure to check. Having said this, throughout the majority of the country you are allowed to name your child whatever you wish.

It's worth remembering that some words may be disallowed for use as a last name, under the same laws that govern first names. As just one example, in Australia, under the *Births, Deaths and Marriages Registration Act* a registrar may be able to refuse to register a name if:

- it's obscene or offensive
- it cannot be established by repute or usage
- it's too long
- it contains symbols without phonetic significance, such as an exclamation or question mark
- it's contrary to public interest

- it contains an official title or rank recognized in Australia such as King, Lady, Father, Sir or Admiral.

Some of these limitations seem arbitrary and subjective to me (lots of new last names, especially combined or blended names, would be unable to established by "repute or usage"; what does "public interest" mean?; also, how long is "too long"?!) but your country's rules on first names may be worth keeping in mind if, for example, you want to make up an entirely new name for your child.

Remember that, in 2016, chosen last names are still a relatively new concept for a large portion of our society. But while bureaucracies and institutions may lag behind, the larger movement of English-speaking countries is towards giving us greater choice for last names.

The Convention on the Elimination of All Forms of Discrimination against Women (CEDAW)—United Nations 1979

I loved discovering the existence of this important document, which states that, in an effort to create "a non-discriminating culture" ... "Women and men, specifically husband and wife, have the same rights to choose a family name."

That was written in 1979 and has since been ratified by 189 states. Australia ratified it in 1983, and the United Kingdom did in 1986. (The United States is yet to ratify

CEDAW, along with only Iran, Somalia, Sudan, the Holy See (Vatican), and Tonga.)

So at least for those in the United Kingdom and Australia, keep in mind that you have these powerful, decades-old words of CEDAW backing up your decision to discuss the matter of what last name your child will have together as a couple.

6

CULTURAL VARIATIONS

It's fascinating to look into other countries' naming traditions, and see the many working last name options at use around the world today. Some cultures didn't opt to use last names until quite recently, while others have quite rigid rules about them. Not every country uses a common last name within families.

- The period in Turkish history just after WWI saw many dramatic reforms to Turkish society, as part of Kemal Ataturk's post-war Westernization movement, but my favourite one is the introduction of the Surname Law, when Turks had to choose their own surnames. Before 1934, Turks didn't have last names, and now they were suddenly forced to choose one out of thin air, so they could take almost any word they wanted to use as a last name. This led to some creative last names, such as Sahin

(hawk), Yildirim (thunderbolt), Simsek (lightning) and Dogan (falcon).
- In the Netherlands parents can choose to give their children either their father's or mother's family name, as long as the parents are married or are living together and the father has acknowledged the child. The last name of any younger siblings must be the same as the last name of the oldest child.
- In Iceland there is no family name; the last name changes with women and men and across generations. They are patronymic, or occasionally matronymic, with part of a person's last name including their father's name. So for example, if a father's name is Erik, then his son's last name would be Eriksson (or Erik's son), and his daughter's last name would be Eriksdottir (or Erik's daughter).
- In Mexico, Latin America and Spain, the children's last name is generally made up of two surnames, referring to each of the parental families. As a result, there are very few common last names; they change with every generation. The first last name is usually the father's family name (or, more precisely, the last name he gained from his father) and the second last name is the mother's family name (or, again, the last name she gained from her father). When last names are passed down through the generations, the father's last name (the first last name) eventually eliminates the

mother's last names from the lineage, because their children and their children's children will only keep the first (paternal) last name for each generation. But while it has been the tradition to observe the paternal-maternal surname order, contemporary law does allow the maternal name to be come first instead if the couple chooses.
- Until 2014, Belgium law insisted that all children be given their father's last name. But the law has changed, and now Belgians have the choice to use either parent's last name, or a combination of both.
- In France, whatever last name is given to the first child must be given to the subsequent children of the same two parents. The law was changed in 2005 allowing parents, whether married or not, to choose the last name of their child. But there are limitations. Couples have the choice of giving the last name of the father, the last name of the mother, or the two last names, hyphenated, in either order. And once chosen, the last name may not be changed. If the couple choose a hyphenated name, only one half of the name can be passed down to the next generation.
- In India, there is a trend towards discarding last names that are synonymous with caste names; instead, people are bestowing brand new last names upon themselves and starting their family history anew.

- China suffers from a huge gender imbalance as a result of sex-selective abortions and the one-child policy. Female infanticide and the abandoning of baby girls have been reported and, in 2012, China had nearly 118 male births for every 100 females. (In most countries, males only slightly outnumber females, with between 103 and 107 boys born for every 100 girls.). In Changfeng county, that ratio has reached nearly 130 boys for every 100 girls. According to a 2014 news article in the *Jianghuai Morning Post* officials in that province decided to give 1000 yuan (USD$150) to couples who take part in the "surname reform" plan, in which parents are enticed to pass on the name of the mother instead. The government hopes to gradually change the common perception that giving birth to a son is preferable to having a daughter. "Our goal is to promote an idea—for families to give their newborn child the last name of whoever they want," a spokesperson said.

7

CH-CH-CH-CH-CHANGES

When we are choosing a last name for our children, it can seem like an immense, make-or-break decision. But let's not forget that people change their last name for lots of reasons, and that it could happen at any stage of life.

Marriage

I changed from my maiden name to my married name then divorced and changed back to my maiden name, then remarried and changed to my married name.

—Tanya Greenbank, mother of Andrew, Samara and Morgan Golding, and Shiloh and Saige Greenbank.

I changed my family name to my wife's family name at

marriage. This was done officially and now my current qualifications, my citizenship certificate etc. use this name.

—Mark Kaneko, father of Ayaka Kaneko

When we got married my partner and I agreed to legally take on the other partner's last name so we would have a shared family name. A big part of this was knowing that we wanted kids and having the sense that sharing a family name was important to us. I wanted to feel like we "belonged" together, and having a shared name achieved that in my mind. When we took on our shared name (Singleton Norton) we both felt like it was an imperfect solution to our struggle to find a compromise that worked for us. I resented my maiden name's ties to my father, but hated the idea of just taking on my partner's last name as it rankled with my feminism. My partner hated the idea of choosing a new last name. I didn't want to be the only one in the pair to "take on" the other name, so I asked my partner if he would take mine as well. He agreed, but was self-conscious about what people would think and say (mostly his family).

—Lefa Singleton Norton, mother of Avery Singleton Norton

I like having a different name to my mother (who has remarried). I like explaining our slightly complex history. It's a nice way to bring it up. I think the same could be said for children with different names. It becomes an interesting part of their story.

—Laura Jean McKay, married

Choice

I shortened my last name from a hyphenated name to a single last name.

—Elyse Truex, mother of Leon Truex

My husband switched his first and middle name officially ... As his father had done too.

—Amelia Chappelow, mother of Felix Chappelow

When my mother married my adoptive dad we both changed our last names. I was eight and it was my choice. I stand strongly by that choice twenty years later.

—Lucinda Vainer, mother of Andrew Lake

My ex changed his last name—the last name he had was his stepdad's last name and he changed it to free himself from all the history (and misery) attached to that name.

—Michelle Brown, mother of Aiesha and Alani Baiden

Known as...

I use my middle name as my last name professionally, which is also my great-grandmother's last name, Carolan. It's an Irish last name and the last name I gave my daughter.

—Renae Whale, mother of Avery Carolan

My official/legal last name is Eldridge, but I go by "Wadsworth" in work and daily life.

—Ann Wadsworth, mother of Daisy, Oscar and Ernest Eldridge

8

TALKING WITH YOUR PARTNER ABOUT LAST NAMES

My partner and I were slow to have the conversation. The long hours spent musing over my future baby's first name had been going on since I was a kid, but I hadn't properly thought about my child's last name until I was actually pregnant, when it suddenly became very real.

I admire couples that have the foresight to think about it early on in their courtship. But it doesn't matter at what point it comes up, it's just important that at some stage it does. Many couples talk through various options for their child, and "try ideas on" for a while to see how they feel. With nine months to think about it, there is usually plenty of time to see if an option works before you have to commit to it.

We agreed pretty early on in our relationship that we didn't need to ever get married—neither of us feel strongly about it. We were pretty young when we met and we didn't really talk about having children for at least the first ten years of our relationship. Then when we did talk about it, it was only because we had so much pressure from friends and family. We still just weren't ready as we were both really enjoying our careers, but we knew that we wanted to have kids one day, so we made a plan that we would definitely start having kids in 2015 ... providing that we didn't get clucky earlier. This was probably the time that I first raised the issue of whose name our child would take—I had been somewhat surprised at the fact that none of our friends had had a discussion about this.

As it happens, I started getting clucky circa 2012. When I finally stopped denying it to myself, I decided that we had to get serious about the last name discussion before we had the child. Our last name negotiations probably put off procreation for another full year. We discussed all available options including a portmanteau (Mastheads? Binsters?), alternating last names for kids (just not fair for them), or Pete taking my name ("that's not an option"). It got to the point where I made it clear that I would just hold out longer than Pete who was fast approaching forty: until I got my way, he would not get any kids.

It was feeling really dysfunctional that we just couldn't agree. Pete was starting to give in, but as soon as he did, I suddenly felt a huge amount of guilt about "winning"—I hated that it had become a competitive process and that someone was going to have to "lose". Very uncharacteristically, I suddenly worried about what other people might think. I am a pretty assertive person and I couldn't get past the fact that this would make people think that Pete and I are not equal partners in the relationship and it would affect our parenting life together. I just didn't think that we're culturally in a place yet where I wouldn't be looked on as dominating if the child took my name.

Sadly, my body clock was ultimately stronger than my stubbornness. My body was telling me it needed to have kids; we needed to end the discussion. I did consider a friend's advice to just get pregnant and hold out until the delivery room when Pete would turn to me, holding our newborn, with tears in his eyes and say, "We can call it anything you want". But I'm just not that kind of girl. So we reached an agreement—the child could take his last name, but he gets no say in the other names. [Mary ended up giving her son her last name as one of his middle names.]

I still don't think we've made the best decision, but I feel that it was ultimately the only decision for us. I guess this is the first of a lifetime to come of mother guilt.

I'm going to make it clear to our kids in the future that it wasn't just a given that they have their dad's name and that it's a discussion we had—I hope I can come up with a better story in the future than just "I got clucky". Hopefully my child doesn't face these same issues when he has kids in the future and it doesn't have to be a "fight", it can just be a genuine and open discussion about what would be best for the child and the family.

—Mary Masters, mother of Gideon Binstead

We thought about using my partner's name, making up a last name for all of us (or using a nice name from either maternal line), just using a first and a middle name (which would then become the last name), but the last two ideas were a bit whacky probably for both of us.

—Linda Roberts, mother of Lev and Zadie Roberts

During the pregnancy but before we knew the sex of the baby, we decided to give the baby the last name of the same sex parent [if it's a boy, he would have the father's last name, and a girl would have the mother's], and for any future siblings to share the same last name.

—Eva Ruggiero, mother of Harper and Ani Johnson

We discussed in the year leading up to pregnancy, and when I became pregnant it was confirmed.

—Sandra Pitcher, mother of Tess Manwaring and Matilda Pitcher

---

Lots of conversations, from as soon as we got pregnant. It was an unplanned pregnancy, so names weren't discussed any earlier.

—Ellen Angus, mother of Georgina Mant

We discussed prior to pregnancy.

—Anthony Fisk, father of Celeste Fisk

I am now at an age where many of my friends are getting married and having children. As a result, my partner and I often discuss the issue of baby names and what we would like to do in our own situation. We have explored the range of options you mention [father's last name, mother's last name, hyphenated last name, alternating last names, blended last name or new name], and they are honestly all on the table. What I know for sure is that we will not default to my (father's) last name for all of the kids, as this doesn't seem right to either of us.

—Andrew Webster, in a relationship

He knows we won't just be defaulting to his last name, so it gets tricky to work out what to do beyond that.

—Sommer Tothill, married

We are twenty-three and twenty-four ... nooooo baby talk yet.

—Bri Lee, in a relationship

Before we began [the process of trying to get pregnant] I raised the last name issue because it was very important to me that we were both on the same page about it.

—Nikki Lusk, mother of Zoë Summers

We didn't arrive at a specific tendency either way, although my initial idea of alternating last names was shot down pretty comprehensively. (I was like "kids will work it out", she was like "I want them to be part of a family. Also, that is an administrative nightmare.") My middle name is my mother's maiden name (God, that's a terrible phrase), so I can imagine us doing something like that rather than hyphenating, although as to whether that's [my name then hers] or hers then mine, we don't yet know.

—Luke Ryan, married

We've discussed this. At first my fella was all, hell no [to an unconventional choice]. Twenty-four hours later he came back to me and said that expecting the father to claim last name rights was patriarchal BS. If we ever do have kids we'd discuss it again and perhaps find a way to include both last names. But I think if a woman carries a baby inside her for forty weeks, she's earned the last name rights.

—Lara Murray, in a relationship

The subtext of the conversations was the precarious (and failing) state of our relationship. Talking about names was a clear reference to the future (that we weren't going to share! And the "family" we weren't going to be). I've always been a committed feminist and my child's father isn't! I think the issue was particularly fraught for him because he has two children from a previous relationship and they don't have his last name so, even though he was pretty ambivalent about the actual baby he might have felt like this was his chance to pass on his name (he didn't articulate this feeling though!)

—Sarah Baker, mother of June Baker

I would have to spend some time reassuring my partner that I really don't have a desire to pass my last name onto the kid.

—Alex Campbell, in a relationship

Who has a better last name? Who has more of a "claim" for their name? Whose last name sounds better with our preferred baby first names? What wasn't discussed but was on both of our minds was, "How would we explain using my last name to your parents when they were already challenged by my decision to keep my own last name when we married?"

—Ellen Angus, mother of Georgina Mant

Ryan comes from a family whose ideology was that women change their last names to become part of the family. I made it known early on that my last name was particularly important to me, not just because of its cultural significance, but also because my father passed away when I was young, and I have always felt that my last name connects me to him, and keeps his spirit alive.

—Mayatili Marika, mother of Thomas and Tessa Griffin

[We were] both flexible. The person (baby) is more important than the name.

—Renee Mills, mother of Ari and Elvie Mahoney

We are in a same-sex relationship and used the family name to show the connection between our son and me (his non-biological parent), and then when I got pregnant with our second, we thought it was more important for the siblings to share a name.

—Rachel Cowling, mother of Fergus and Evie Cowling

[My partner] was not very worried about the last name of our prospective kids, whereas I was more preoccupied with getting

it "right" and giving them a last name that symbolized their origins and connections.

—Pia Cerveri, mother of Ori and Arlo Cerveri-Ward

We try not to "do" difficult. We mostly tell each other what we think and then ponder that. I'm cool with how it turned out.

—Andrea Innocent, mother of Luc Jacobs

I would love my children to be Lushes. I realize it is more than likely I will need to compromise on this through hyphenation or the blending of names.

—Amelia Lush, single

[Things we might discuss include] patriarchal traditions, family pressure to follow cultural conventions, neither partner wishing to pass their name on (or both wishing to), and language barriers (choosing a name that works in multiple languages).

—Jane Greenbank, single

[Such a decision for us involves negotiating] the merits of both

names, going against social expectation and constantly justifying choice (especially for him who doesn't feel as strongly about the issue). [I would also consider my] in-laws with traditional ideas who are already wary of me and may take offense.

—Ellie Higgins, in a relationship

11

HELP! WE DON'T KNOW WHICH LAST NAME TO USE!

The Six Last Name Options

Now, it's time to really talk and begin the process of trying to work out which last name might work best for your family. It's an important conversation (or more likely, series of conversations), because besides just coming to a decision about your baby's last name, it can also set up the standards and expectations by which you wish to parent your child. It's a conversation that will necessarily bring out your beliefs and value systems, and knowing these things about your partner can help forge a strong basis for your parenting life together.

I

OPTION 1: FATHER'S LAST NAME

To say that men are more likely to expect their children to have their last name is hardly controversial. It's an expectation that goes way back through Western culture, to the law of coverture. And even though "wives" are not technically seen as vassals, or under the husband's control or protection, anymore, the majority of men in our society tend to grow up not really giving the last name issue a second thought.

Passing on the father's last name is by far the most common choice for most heterosexual couples with different last names in the United States, United Kingdom and Australia, and it still remains an ideal choice for many people.

. . .

The kids have my husband's name. It's just easier. [I'm] not keen on hyphenated names.

—Renee Mills, mother of Ari and Elvie Mahoney

We decided it would have caused too much controversy in my family had he not been given my last name.

—Sam Scriba, father of Ari Scriba

I preferred our daughter have her father's name, as it's shorter and not ethnic like mine.

—Joanna Peppas, mother of Jennifer Gray

We decided it was important for all the kids to have the same last name.

—Melanie Wallis, mother of Nathan and Emily Burns

I felt it important that my partner felt attached to the baby, as we weren't married and it had always been me who really wanted children.

—Jo Turner, mother of Toby, Phoebe and Max Luce

[It] seemed easiest to stick with tradition just to avoid paperwork complexities, people getting the wrong idea about home relationship etc.

—Myles Cuffe, father of Senan, Leonore and Luan Cuffe

The Yolngu live in a patrilineal society, in which each individual takes their identity, last name, clan group, cultural responsibilities and traditional land ownership from their father and grandfather. So, women always have a different last name from their children and husband. Therefore, I had no qualms about my children having their father's last name. Even thought he is not Indigenous, I still wanted to carry on this Yolngu tradition. He was happy that our children would have his last name.

—Mayatili Marika, mother of Thomas and Tessa Griffin

She was born in Thailand, which only recognized her surrogate mother and biological father (me). There was no recognition of [my partner] Joseph. When you are trying to leave a foreign country it is best to make it easier and reduce complications.

—Anthony Fisk, father of Celeste Fisk

Ours is a nice name and I just assumed we would all have the same name as a family. A little old-fashioned maybe.

—Patricia Berrington, married

It was something I decided, as I had no attachment to my own [last name] for my children, but loved my partner's name.

—Lee Sandwith, mother of Sailor and Rio Christmass

In the end it came down to cultural identity. And while calling her Nguyen will open up a whole can of worms for her in dealing with other people's expectations as she grows up, we thought that in the long run it would be good for Georgette to have that connection to her heritage. On her mother's side of the family, she is a seventh or eighth generation Australian, but on my side she is the second generation.

—Hop Dac Nguyen, father of Georgette Nguyen

My brother has children with our family name and my husband's side of the family has no children yet—it felt right for his family. I am still considering changing my name down the track to my husband's, but I will also see what my son thinks about us having different names as he gets older.

—Louise Coulthard, mother of Alexander Fitzpatrick

It was important to my partner and didn't bother me. Fairly simple.

—Rebecca Slack, mother of Luca Hagenson

It really was a no-brainer for us. I wanted the baby to have his last name and not mine. Also, my partner is the last male with his family name, so if we had a boy it meant that his last name would be passed on. I'm glad [our son] is able to carry on my partner's family name. I know this may sound old-fashioned, but it wasn't out of old-fashioned beliefs that I chose this way. If I had changed my name back to my birth last name, the choice may not have been so easy for me. I may have chosen to incorporate my name as well as my partner's in some way.

—Melissa Carter, mother of Finlay Inglis

It just sounded good with the first name we chose. And I expect it is tradition. I also wanted to give that to my husband, rather than insist on my own last name. And we still might have my name for the next child!

—Paula Morreau, mother of Sage Robertson

We chose the last name that went best with the first name we wanted! Ha!

—Clare Chippendale, mother of Ginger Rogers

Although Pete doesn't feel a deep connection with his family name, he did lose his dad and so there was the idea of continuing on with it in honor of him. Also that Pete comes from a small family and I come from an enormous one, so there's more chance that the Hart name will be preserved! We didn't want to hyphenate either, purely based on aesthetics. Maybe we thought it looked a bit pompous or something! Also I guess there's always the chance that Pete and I will get married and although I would always keep my maiden name, it would mean Baxter is the official family name. I do sometimes regret not including my last name somewhere in Fox's name. Even [if] it was a second middle name ... I think we would have if it sounded better. In the end Fox Miró Baxter Hart sounded better to us than Fox Miró Hart Baxter so we just decided to drop Hart altogether.

—Sunni Hart, mother of Fox Baxter

I took Glenn's last name so that Eddie, Glenn and I would all have the same last name.

—Laura Rees, mother of Edward Rees

We chose my partner's last name, as it is more likely than mine to become "extinct", as my brother was trying for a child (and his wife changed to Jaffe) and my partner's brother is gay and has no interest in having children.

—Ilana Jaffe, mother of Abe Hoffman

We spent a lot of time thinking about our child's first name, almost no time discussing last names.

—Sari Fordham, mother of Kai Bradford

Sharp is cooler than Heap!

—Lexington Heap, mother of Oliver and Lilith Sharp

We will be getting married, so we wanted to share the same last name. I gave [my son] the middle name Peter as a nod to my family—Peters.

—Kimberley Peters, mother of Angus Baxter

It's just tradition.

—Bronwyn Sutton, mother of Hermione Ferguson

For us, it wasn't a conflict-ridden issue. Obviously, for me it was an emotional decision—a rejection of my father—but it wasn't something we sweated over.

—Jessie Cole, mother of Milla and Luca Finardi

We decided that the main pros for my name were being top of the alphabetical list (Angus) and also that it was a bold choice and we'd like to instill the values behind that choice in our future children. The main pros for his name were: it sounded better with our chosen first names; he was the only Mant from his family in the country, whereas I am related to lots of Anguses; similarly, that the baby would have a close relationship with my local family and a distant one with his, so it would be nice to let them have that connection (or more specifically, not to take that connection away, as his family would never have expected anything different); and that my brother had already had a baby Angus, but [my partner's] sister hadn't kept her last name, meaning that there would be no more Mants in his family. Also I think deep down we knew it would just be easier. As a compromise, we agreed to alternate last names with siblings after using his first. (Now that our daughter is three and a second one is on the way, we have given up on that compromise, but are considering Angus as a first name.)

—Ellen Angus, mother of Georgina Mant

He decided. There was no discussion. It was instantly assumed they would have his name. If I'd even mentioned that I was considering giving the girls my name he would've made my life miserable until I gave in. That says more about the relationship than it does about his valuing the meaning of names, though. I think there was an element of ego attached to him wanting them to have his name; I think it also gave him a feeling of ownership over the kids.

—Michelle Brown, mother of Aiesha and Alani Baiden

We've discussed it in a way. There is more family heritage linked to my fiancé's name, and I think it is important to him that our children carry his name. We haven't ever discussed it in detail because I'm happy to go along with that—not because I feel that it should be the male whose name is used, but because I like the idea of the whole family having the same name, and his last name is cooler sounding than mine. If I had already published extensively under my current name, I would probably feel differently though. Hyphenated last names just seem like a pain to always be spelling out, especially over the phone.

—Brooke Sharpley, in a relationship

[The decision was] automatic, [in a] post-birth haze.

—Natalie Birdsley, mother of Christopher and Hazel O'Connor

I hate patriarchy, but to be honest it's probably easier to stick to convention and go with dad's last name for the kids.

—Angela May, single

1

ISSUES TO CONSIDER WITH THIS OPTION

Duty

If you're the only male in the family you might feel a responsibility to pass on your last name. "But, I must!" you say. "It's my duty." When you come from a long line where every son has carried on the family name, it can feel like a heavy and important burden that isn't worth fighting against.

But it should also be noted, for argument's sake, that family names have often changed over the generations, to suit the times, for convenience or ease, or to advance socially. Last names belong to each individual, and there is a good case to be made that they can be molded to fit the times in which that individual lives. Dig a few generations back and you're likely to find that your great-great-grandfather whose name you proudly carry on didn't actually have that name at birth.

If you want to find out the facts for yourself, instead of

relying on family hearsay and mythology it's very easy these days to research your own family history online and discover more details about the last name you feel obliged to continue to use. You might be surprised.

We both have strong opinions. His family expects their last name.

—Justine Arentz, in a relationship

Future generations

Despite the conversations we have about the times a changin', many couples still think in terms of having sons who will pass on their last name. This is by no means a given, and in twenty or thirty years when your kids are having kids, your sons may not feel the necessity to pass their last name on to their children at all.

I recognize there is a touch of melancholy associated with this; some traditions can be beautiful and reassuring things. But the function of last names has changed so significantly that parents today have to take this possibility on board. The last name choice they make may not have the same significance it once had for the continuation of a bloodline, so if this is the only reason why you are passing on the father's last name, it's worth thinking over.

What message are you sending?

Part of your discussion with your partner might include what message you're sending to your children. Our kids learn how to behave in the world from us, their parents. So it's worth considering whether you'd feel comfortable making a choice that favors men's history over women's, or if there might be a way to incorporate more of a balance.

Chris was so certain of the fact that our son was getting the last name. So we compromised and gave our son my dad's name as his middle name. We also discussed that if we ever have a girl she would have her middle name after my mother.

—Rebecca Stock, mother of Logan Galea

We had hypothetical conversations, years before having a baby, which were revisited once I fell pregnant. We both assumed, actually, that any baby/babies we'd have would take Jon's last name. I had also decided, and Jon agreed, that our child/children would also be given my last name (Murphy), as their middle name. That way, they carry both our names.

—Kathleen Murphy, mother of Molly Wardle

Family unity

While it's extremely common these days for a woman to have a different last name to her children, some women say they worry about not being recognized as the mother if their kids have the father's last name. If this reflects your feelings, you might want to consider whether you'll eventually change your last name to match that of the rest of your family.

If the question of family unity is important to you, another solution could be to use the mother's last name for the children (which means the father will have a different last name instead—see Option 2).

Evans was the easy way. We had what seemed like a good reason to want a single family name ... envisioning the family, fleeing as refugees ... separated ... reunited by the UNHCR due to a name. Lame. I know. We lived in Byron Shire [northern New South Wales in Australia]. No way we were going down the invented name route—the wrecks lay all around us.

—Thomas Evans, father of Maya and Tashi Evans

I don't understand when women say that they want to change their last name so that their whole family has the same name, because they want to have a sense of family, etc. If you're not part of the family if you change your name, does that mean you're no longer in your parents' family? It's nonsensical.

—Sum Ambepitiya, married

Social, family and your own expectations

You're not going to get much objection to this choice. Giving your child their father's last name will allow you to sail under the radar, and not have to deal with any "unpleasant" discussions, relaxing safe in the knowledge you are among the 90 per cent of families who have made the same decision.

But while you are unlikely to come up against many external barriers to your decision, it's worth discussing together what your interior responses are.

Many people, until they think about it, won't have any strong feelings, because we have been brought up to not question such conventions. You might be surprised to find your partner does consider it antiquated after all, but just assumed it was "the done thing". Hopefully this book will demonstrate that there are many other options out there, which are becoming more common.

You might feel some (and most probably, it will be silent) judgment from those in your family and social group who believe that society should be trying to redress the imbalance of gender inequality, but this will depend on the community you live in.

2

DISCUSSING THIS OPTION WITH YOUR PARTNER

There are many different anxieties around last names. Whether you're discussing equality, identity, aesthetics, or extended family, you are probably opening a can of worms when you open up this conversation.

My advice is: let it all out. Both of you should put all your worries and anxieties out on the table, without fear of judgment, and then you'll be able to see what you have to work with.

The day we decided to start trying [for a baby] we went out to dinner to kind of celebrate and I said straight out that the baby would have his last name. I knew it was very important to him for the baby to have his name, and I didn't want my last name being passed on.

—Melissa Carter, mother of Finlay Inglis

I can't remember when we first talked about it, but it was before I was pregnant and we had decided that [the baby] would probably take Hop's last name. He was okay with it having both, or discussing it just having mine, but given the baby was going to be living so far away from its Vietnamese family members, we wanted it to have a connection to its Vietnamese heritage. We knew it would likely have an Anglo first name, so giving her Hop's last name seemed like a good way to honor her family culture.

—Kate Harris, mother of Georgette Nguyen

The conversation that was difficult for me was explaining how I felt like my son wasn't going to carry on anything from my side of the family, especially as he could never meet my mother and father. I wanted him to have some part of his name as a reminder, so he can feel like they would have loved him.

—Rebecca Stock, mother of Logan Galea

There weren't really any difficult conversations between us, but I had a conversation with the pediatrician while in hospital and she suggested that I consider other alternatives because Avery's father and I weren't in a relationship and I didn't know what the future would hold. I'm glad I had that conver-

sation with her, and it helped me make a decision that both [my daughter's] father and I are happy with.

—Renae Whale, mother of Avery Carolan

[The discussion] was about what sounded better. A name that could be lived up to as an identity in a world that vastly values recognition of brand and self-image. Middle names were a tribute to [my] heritage and [their] last name to his.

—Lee Sandwith, mother of Sailor and Rio Christmass

It wasn't open for discussion. They were always going to be called Baiden. I felt a little off about it—but the promise of marriage in the future led me to imagine that eventually I would change my name so the girls and I would all have the same name.

—Michelle Brown, mother of Aiesha and Alani Baiden

I was always adamant that I would never change my last name. The trade-off was that if we had children, they would have their father's last name. We discussed this many times, and from early on in our relationship.

—Mayatili Marika, mother of Thomas and Tessa Griffin

We never discussed a "double-barrel" name because I think it's a conceit to think a child needs to go about representing the names of the parents, and combining is untenable when the names accumulate through marriage. In any case, my [current] partner Martin should rightfully be included in the mix as he's parented Daniel for eight years (of twelve). A triple (or more) last name takes the problem to a logical extreme.

—Anna Gottstein, mother of Daniel Archer

I agreed that the kids could share his name even if I didn't. It was a compromise because I think he was slightly disappointed when I didn't take his name.

—Carly Cook, mother of Charles, Louis and George Berghofer

It was super casual. Neither of us wanted our child to have a hyphenated name. I was happy for our child to take Bradford and my husband was happy for our child to take Fordham. Tradition won.

—Sari Fordham, mother of Kai Bradford

During pregnancy we discussed it, and both agreed he would be a Birchall pretty quickly ... It's only since he was born that we've realized it's odd to be a family with different names.

—Ben Birchall, father of Walter Birchall

I had already changed my name to his, so it was an easy decision (though that did have bearing on me changing my name initially—I wanted for us all to share the same last name when we had kids).

—Jessica Worrall, mother of Elise Worrall

Basically I definitely wanted them to have his last name and then I was worried about keeping my *last name because I thought people might think I was "the other woman" when picking the kids up from school! ... And I'd say I disagree with people using say, just the mother's last name for the children's last name! Maybe I have issues, haha—but I'd say it should be the husband's last name or a combination of both.*

—Ann Wadsworth, mother of Daisy, Oscar and Ernest Eldridge

It didn't seem fair that the mother didn't get to pass on a name. It bothered me more than her.

—Myles Cuffe, father of Senan, Leonore and Luan Cuffe

My biggest issue was having a different last name as my daughter (since [my partner and I] are not married). When asked whether he would be fine having a different last name to [our daughter], he was very much against it. Even though I made the point that if we were going to be married eventually it shouldn't matter—at some point she would change to Milne. He still hated the idea and was firmly against it. I suppose I just had to give in ... and a big part of me didn't want to (a) give her a hyphenated last name or (b) give her a last name that she will need to go through the trouble of changing at some point in her life.

—Darcy Laughlin, mother of Emily Milne

We would have liked a hyphenated last name but Chippendale-Rogers is a bit long. Neither of us had a strong feeling but we wanted something that felt right.

—Clare Chippendale, mother of Ginger Rogers

I guess it was assumed that our child would take my last name, but we did discuss hypothetically him getting her last name.

—Sam Scriba, father of Ari Scriba

We had a lot of trouble agreeing on first names, but the last name, not so much. I think I saw my own last name as being a signifier of my father, who, at that stage, I was very angry with. I felt no inner pressure to carry on his name, or to show him respect, in fact probably quite the opposite. I also felt that, aesthetically, mixing such an "Anglo" name with an Italian name, as would happen in a hyphenation, would look and sound silly, and that mattered to me at that age. I'm fairly sure my partner would have been happy to do whatever I liked, as long as his name was included. I think I purposely chose to leave off my own last name out of anger towards my dad. My own parents had never married, so my mother always had her own separate name, so I associated my last name entirely with my dad, not with "the family".

—Jessie Cole, mother of Milla and Luca Finardi

It was complicated. Neither of us wanted to take the other person's last name—double-barrelled last names seem inappropriate for men, especially with two different cultural backgrounds. We decided Celeste would take her biological father's last name and her egg donor's name as a middle name (who is also [my partner] Joseph's sister).

—Anthony Fisk, father of Celeste Fisk

There were a few factors: (1) There are many Winterbottoms (my father is from a family of twelve). I love my last name but I knew it wasn't going to disappear if it wasn't used. (2) Manson is less common and Matthieu is from a much smaller family. His sisters have been married and have changed their names so it is just him and his brother who would retain the last name in their immediate family. (3) We didn't know if the baby would be male or female. We waited until he was born and after some time named him (six weeks). The first name had to fit with the last name and middle names (obviously) but we were still open to using both names. Double barreling wasn't an option as we'd both thought that would be clumsy. "Winterbottom-Manson" doesn't roll off the tongue that easily.

—Dana Winterbottom, mother of Ornette Manson

We considered giving her my name, but we were also going through visa issues so we thought best to link it to my partner.

—Jasmin Tulk, mother of Maryam Avanaki

Chris would have been fine with my last name, and I mentioned we could make a completely new one, but I think in the end it was better to keep the family connection there, given we had done years of IVF and had had the support of everyone, emotionally and financially.

—Andrea Innocent, mother of Luc Jacobs

My partner wouldn't entertain the idea of me passing on my last name even though he comes from a matriarchal tradition. I think this is because his father was largely absent from his childhood and he believes giving our child his name is a strong sign of his involvement.

—Megan Parker, mother of Iris O'Neill

We wanted to have the same name, and for our kids to also share that name. But neither of us especially wanted to change our name, and the option of inventing a name seemed twee. If I changed my name to Wilson, my old man would be deeply hurt. If we went conventional, with Evans, nobody would bat an eyelid when Steph changed her name, or when the kids presented as little Evanses. Old Mrs Wilson had been calling her daughter Mrs Evans for years. Lame, I know.

—Thomas Evans, father of Maya and Tashi Evans

We never wanted to hyphenate them and his father in particular really wanted the child to be a Jacobs to carry on the family name. Under my breath I was all like, "It's not Game of Thrones, *mate."*

—Andrea Innocent, mother of Luc Jacobs

How do I know it's my kid?

Women know the baby is theirs, having given birth to it. For men, passing their last name on to their child gives them a link, and reassures them that this child is related to them. While this is hardly ever the explicit reason for both men and women wanting to pass on the father's last name, it's important to acknowledge the societal distrust of women that still permeates some of our ancient rituals and traditions. Unless they choose the father's last name, women might feel concerned society will view them unfavorably (to put it more succinctly—they might fear being slut-shamed), and men might feel that the last name is a crucial way to assert and display their paternity.

All of this heavy weight of history is bound to affect your thinking on this matter, and it will be extremely helpful during your conversations to try to untangle some of your views on this matter and find out where they're coming from. Social conditioning works on us all!

3

DIFFICULTIES (OR LACK OF) RESULTING FROM THIS CHOICE

No last name option is truly perfect: difficult or annoying situations may arise with any of the choices you choose, depending on your personality type and the community you live in. For example, even the seemingly foolproof option of giving your kids the father's last name may cause difficulties for the mother if she has a different last name.

I'm nervous about traveling overseas with her having a different last name to mine.

—Joanna Peppas, mother of Jennifer Gray

I get really annoyed when people assume it's my family name too. His family refused to accept that I never took it. Mail came incorrectly addressed. Nurses couldn't find me in the hospital. I mean, really. How hard is it to understand?

—Emily Goode, mother of Arlo, Bertrand and Lyle Godfrey

I think institutions are much more used to couples having different names now. Peter's family will send things to Melanie Burns even though we have never married.

—Melanie Wallis, mother of Nathan and Emily Burns

It seems quite common. But I do always feel odd explaining that the kids don't have the same name as me.

—Michelle Brown, mother of Aiesha and Alani Baiden

Sometimes it can be difficult. Particularly when traveling, as boarding passes have different last names. Also, Medicare cards, passports, posed some challenges. Also, just the conversations that arise.

—Mayatili Marika, mother of Thomas and Tessa Griffin

I often get called Mahoney. Sometimes it makes others uncom-

fortable ... Not me though.

—Renee Mills, mother of Ari and Elvie Mahoney

Our daughter has the same name as an old Hollywood film star. We get some comments but I have lived as a Chippendale my whole life so we can deal.

—Clare Chippendale, mother of Ginger Rogers

[I've had difficulties] a couple of times because she has a different last name to me. It's quickly fixed.

—Bronwyn Sutton, mother of Hermione Ferguson

It's just mainly correcting their assumptions but it's never too bad.

—Sunni Hart, mother of Fox Baxter

It makes it more complicated at school to have a name that is different to my kids. Sometimes I just get called Mrs Berghofer anyway, which doesn't bother me. As a teacher, different last names are more and more common and therefore more acceptable.

—Carly Cook, mother of Charles, Louis and George Berghofer

Getting on a plane [was problematic]. Tom had to be the parent in charge because [our children] share [his] last name.

—Lexington Heap, mother of Oliver and Lilith Sharp

In the first few months at check-ups I kept missing his name as it was called out, expecting to hear mine.

—Jessica Friedmann, mother of Owen Baylis

I'm used to saying, "I'm Ellen Angus, Georgie Mant's mum." It's so common to have different last names that nobody questions it. A (white) friend of mine had a baby with her (black) partner and gave her the dad's last name—the baby has very dark skin and looks just like her dad, and my friend hates having a different last name to her. I can understand that, because people already question the relationship when they see them together.

—Ellen Angus, mother of Georgina Mant

My kid looks like a total whitefella. We've had to go to hospital a few times with her and each time we report at the desk and they ask for her last name, my first thought each time is that they're not going to believe she's my daughter. So [when thinking about whether we've faced any difficulties,] I guess the answer is no, nothing beyond my own paranoia.

—Hop Dac Nguyen, father of Georgette Nguyen

[We only had problems once], when I was traveling internationally with [my daughter] on my own (she was three months) I was questioned at customs and asked to produce a birth certificate to prove I was her mother. Annoying.

—Kathleen Murphy, mother of Molly Wardle

[A difficulty we face, with my name being different to my kids', is] receipts in the wrong name.

—Emily Goode, mother of Arlo, Bertrand and Lyle Godfrey

Sometimes I feel people may think I am a single parent because my name is different from my child's.

—Melissa Carter, mother of Finlay Inglis

[There is] occasional awkwardness/difficulty with banks or institutions because [my partner and I are] not married. [We experience a] few extra questions at customs when my sister and I traveled with my baby [who has a different name to us] but not my baby's father.

—Megan Parker, mother of Iris O'Neill

I have two sets of aunts and uncles who are unmarried and have kids. While it's progressive of their Baby Boomers generation to have never been married, I don't think that it would have ever been a discussion for them to not use the father's last name for the children. My cousins have not been affected at all by not having the same last name as their mothers—it's just the usual rigmarole of the mother needing to travel with documentation to prove the children belong to her, or proving to hospital administration that this is her child. I have been known to answer to Mrs Binstead in situations where it wasn't worth correcting, or referring to Pete as my husband rather than boyfriend, and I am sure I will do this with our children.

—Mary Masters, mother of Gideon Binstead

I feel that often when I talk to teachers etc. at my kids' schools (high school in particular) no one ever knows who I am because the connection between me and my kids isn't obvious. That bugs me a little.

—Jessie Cole, mother of Milla and Luca Finardi

My mother kept her maiden name, and we used to get two school reports sent to the same address—one to her and one to my father. Other than minor (usually humorous) confusions, there's been no issues for me.

—Cassie Reynolds, in a relationship

I think there are enough family arrangements going around that nobody questions different last names these days.

—Ellen Angus, mother of Georgina Mant

Growing up with my mother having a different last name to the rest of our family has never been an issue to my knowledge. It has always irritated me that banks and other institutions still set security questions as "What is your mother's maiden name?", because it's the same as her grown-woman-of-sixty name. But that's a small difficulty in the scheme of things.

—Lucy Evans, in a relationship

I suppose it always stung a bit, after my parents got divorced, when I'd see my mother's name on an envelope in the mail, or when one of my friends would call her Mrs McGuire and it wasn't really true anymore.

—Tim McGuire, single

My mother would occasionally get called Mrs Baker (which wasn't her name) by the schools that my brother and I went to but I don't think that it was a huge problem for her.

—Sarah Baker, mother of June Baker

I have a different last name to my mother. I remember people asking why sometimes, but it wasn't difficult. It's different in a world full of step-families/half-families etc. I think.

—Linda Roberts, mother of Lev and Zadie Roberts

My child isn't at school yet but there is sometimes confusion at doctors' appointments. I know my own mother kept her own name until I started school then ended up taking my father's (and my) last name because she felt social pressure having a different name to her children. I started school in 1987.

—Megan Parker, mother of Iris O'Neill

In primary school some people thought it was weird that I had a different last name to my mother when I hadn't met my dad.

(I met him when I was fifteen). Or if I wrote her name on forms I would get asked, "Who is that to you?"

—Rebecca Stock, mother of Logan Galea

I do know of single mothers with children having their absent father's last name, and hanging on to the name themselves to have the same last name as their children, which then means having an ex-husband's last name for the rest of your life. I haven't had any issues personally.

—Elyse Truex, mother of Leon Truex

To avoid [difficulties] is why I wanted the family to have the same name.

—Emily Hall, mother of Mia Hall

We are the only nuclear, uni-named family in the Byron Shire. Stand out like a sore thumb among all the Stream Shakti Nanayas.

—Thomas Evans, father of Maya and Tashi Evans

4

REGRETS (OR LACK OF) ARISING FROM THIS CHOICE

Any last name choice has the potential to be regretted in hindsight. In the case of choosing the father's last name for your child, society is changing very quickly and if you are a progressive in other areas of your life, you might soon feel disappointed that you didn't go with a more progressive last name for your child.

If you're the mother, you might feel regret that your name isn't represented in the name of your child, or that you don't have a nominal connection with your child. By talking these things through beforehand with your partner you will be able to make a better decision, or at least have your feelings on the record so, no matter what the eventual outcome of your conversation might be, there is mutual understanding.

I still can get a bit wistful [because] I feel like I did the hard yards bringing her into the world and keeping her alive for the first months and that it would be a really nice thing to share a name with her, but I'm more attached to my reasons for her having Hop's name.

—Kate Harris, mother of Georgette Nguyen

Sometimes I think about adding mine to our daughter's name for passport and school, but I haven't yet.

—Joanna Peppas, mother of Jennifer Gray

We're both happy with our decision.

—Rebecca Stock, mother of Logan Galea

No [regrets] from my end.

—Ben Birchall, father of Walter Birchall

Yes, [I regret it]. Every day.

—Emily Goode, mother of Arlo, Bertrand and Lyle Godfrey

I think both of us have at times regretted not going for something grand and invented.

—Thomas Evans, father of Maya and Tashi Evans

[I don't regret it], but sometimes it makes me sad I don't have the same family name as my daughter.

—Clare Chippendale, mother of Ginger Rogers

I regret it now. Because I made the choice based on the fact that I thought we would eventually all have the same name once we were married. Instead, the promised proposal never came, he decided to leave, and I'm left feeling a little bit left out. It's rough, when you're doing it mostly on your own and you feel so connected to your little girls, to know that they don't have the same name as you. It doesn't make me feel less connected to them, it's just an endless reminder of all the broken promises. The name is essentially a symbol of the failed relationship that I am so keen to leave behind me. Just another way I'm endlessly attached to a relationship that was fairly crippling for me. And that really bothers me.

—Michelle Brown, mother of Aiesha and Alani Baiden

Yes, I [regret that I] don't feel like one of "the Luces". And the kids have remarked on it.

—Jo Turner, mother of Toby, Phoebe and Max Luce

[I've] only [felt regret] when I'm at the doctors or daycare when I feel strange that we don't share [a last name].

—Sunni Hart, mother of Fox Baxter

I don't regret it but sometimes I feel a little wistful.

—Megan Parker, mother of Iris O'Neill

[I only regretted it] when the kids had to learn how to spell it!

—Carly Cook, mother of Charles, Louis and George Berghofer

I don't regret it. But part of me really hates having a different last name to her.

—Darcy Laughlin, mother of Emily Milne

I automatically gave our first child my partner's last name when filling out the birth certificate. I regretted it and tried to speak to my partner about it but he refused to change it.

—Natalie Birdsley, mother of Christopher and Hazel O'Connor

Sometimes I feel a bit sad that I didn't go with the hyphenated choice. As the years have gone by I've come to identify my last name with me, not my dad, which means I feel a bit sad that my kids don't carry that signifier (or presence) of their mother in their names. But at the same time I really love that they identify with their Italian heritage, and that their name indicates their cultural heritage. I feel like this, partly because my ex's father is a beautiful man, and he has built a very strong family structure here in Australia and I envy and appreciate that, and I am happy that my kids have the benefits of it.

—Jessie Cole, mother of Milla and Luca Finardi

Sometimes I think that I've sold her into a lifetime of being harassed by people about having a Vietnamese last name, but the onus is really on me to help her understand and appreciate the significance of having it.

—Hop Dac Nguyen, father of Georgette Nguyen

II

OPTION 2: MOTHER'S LAST NAME

There are lots of reasons why couples might choose to pass down the mother's last name rather than the father's. For some, it's a deliberately feminist choice; for others it just sounds better. Some men simply don't care as much about their last names as their female partners do, or the decision is made for political reasons.

It was my husband who suggested that our child would have my last name, his reasoning being that I have a much stronger connection to my family and culture through my last name than he does. Also, having a large extended family means that my last name is a connection to this group of people, whereas my husband has a small immediate family and doesn't have contact with any extended family.

At first I was unsure, mainly because my experiences with last names has been fairly "traditional" up until recently, and so I felt like David would be missing out on something by not sharing a last name with his child. But as it was his suggestion, I knew that he was supportive and comfortable, that I wasn't forcing this choice on him.

In the end, I realized that although it is an important decision to make, there are many more choices we will have to make as parents that will create a family bond far stronger than a name alone.

—Sophie Fernandes, mother of "Roo" Fernandes

We thought it sounded better with the first name. Also, we both felt it was a bit of a cop-out going with the father's name. I'd have felt as though I wasn't being true to myself. In the end it just kind of happened.

—Linda Roberts, mother of Lev and Zadie Roberts

We chose a first name we liked and then decided to use the last name that sounded best with the first name, which just happened to be my last name. For our second child it was important to me that she have the same last name as her sister.

—Judy Waugh, mother of Amelia and Fiona Waugh

My husband brought it up first and we probably kissed and

gushed over the baby and felt very giddy. So we just decided Chappelow for [our son] and I feel very happy we are both Chappelows.

—Amelia Chappelow, mother of Felix Chappelow

I chose my last name as I would be the primary care provider as the stay-at-home parent, and I figured that he would be more my child.

—Vu Ngoc Hiep Huynh, mother of Noah Huynh

We decided that she would have both our names, but that my name would be the name that she would use day to day. Her dad's last name is her middle name, and if she wishes to use it (particularly given it connects her to her Maltese heritage), she can.

—Ada Conroy, mother of Pippa Conroy

By the time my daughter was born, I was on my own. It was a no-brainer to give her my last name! I'm so happy I did. I would've really wanted to even if I'd still been with her dad.

—Sarah Baker, mother of June Baker

I'm more interested in equity than in maintaining the family name. We have accurate birth records now; why should we retain an archaic way of determining family relations and paternity? For that reason I'm happy to cede control over any future children's last names to their mother.

—Chad Parkhill, married

I think it's hugely important for women to assert their own names as a way of making non-patronymic naming practices unremarkable.

—Laura Maher, single

I have a friend who took his wife's last name and legally changed his name. Their two children are boys and without taking her last name it wouldn't have carried on in the family as her sisters both have girls.

—Laura Rees, mother of Edward Rees

I don't know any other child with their mother's last name, rather than their father's. For me, it was not about ownership of the child—we mainly refer to her as Maggie Vali [her middle name].

—Lucy Filor, mother of Maggie Filor

A friend of mine has two children by two different men, and the children have the fathers' names. I think this could be hard for the kids at times, and I also think that maybe they should have just had her name. Though because of the society we live in, she didn't feel was like that was an option.

—Tace Kelly, in a relationship

5

ISSUES TO CONSIDER WITH THIS OPTION

Bureaucracy

Bureaucracy can make it difficult when either parent has a different last name to their child, and it's much more uncommon for fathers to have different names to their children than it is for mothers, so you may find yourself explaining it to people. A simple way to be certain your connection to your child is recognized regardless of last name, is to carry a certified copy of their birth certificate in your wallet.

Social and family expectations

Despite many advances in breaking down gender roles, society is still patriarchal. It's possible the father might fear being seen emasculated by his partner. It takes a guy who is confident to push back against this type of, often invisible, societal conditioning, and see it for what it is.

If we lived in a society where the "free" choice was 50/50 then I'd be happy with a 50/50. We don't, so anyone who thinks about it should stand for the minority choice.

—Martin Bush, father of Remi and Aida Oke

I was keen to avoid following the patriarchal tradition of using the man's last name. Daryl could see that point.

—Lucy Filor, mother of Maggie Filor

I didn't change my last name when I got married. I strongly wanted my child to have my last name as I felt that going through pregnancy gave me a greater tie to the baby at that point. Ben wasn't bothered at all so there was no conflict on the matter.

—Daine Singer, mother of Inez Singer

I suspect Chad's parents will be sad if their grandchildren don't have their name ... but really it's only Chad's father's name anyway. And no one would bat an eyelid if we gave our children Chad's name only, so basically I think those concerns are nonsense. Also, Chad will probably object, but I think that men don't get to be feminists/feminist allies without having to actually give up anything. If you're a man who has never had to give up any privilege ever, then I don't think you can call yourself a feminist ally.

—Zora Sanders, married

Strangely enough, it is my parents (the Sri Lankan future grandparents) who will certainly lose their minds when we tell them their grandchild has their last name. My family are very traditional, and very patriarchal, and will think that I've talked my husband into this as some sort of weird stubborn power play, and that it will totally disrespect and anger my white in-laws, who, honestly, I can't imagine really blinking over it.

—Sum Ambepitiya, married

I think my partner and I will be in accord; I suspect her family may be surprised by our decision [to give our child the mother's last name], while mine will be disappointed by it (though are unlikely to make a fuss).

—David Laurence, in a relationship

In my current relationship I think maybe the in-laws would pose more of an issue than my partner. They are French and have a strong family history. They like me and respect me though, and I don't think they'd be able to get too upset if we wanted to split the name between siblings or hyphenate. They'd freak if I only wanted to use my last name though, which is of course, a double standard, because they'd be cool if we only used his ... grrrr.

—Bri Lee, in a relationship

My partner's mother had a very strong reaction, and called us crying at 6am one day, accusing us of trying to exclude her from our baby's life. This was the hardest thing—that she didn't understand or care about the importance of us being able to make decisions that were best for us.

—Ada Conroy, mother of Pippa Conroy

[There were no issues] for me, though I think Ben's parents might have privately told him they disapproved.

—Daine Singer, mother of Inez Singer

We were pretty chilled about the whole thing; however, any time [my partner's] mother's preferences got brought up I obviously wasn't too happy [because she disagreed with our decision].

—Cecilia Acevedo, mother of Silas Acevedo

I maybe felt a small amount of guilt for hogging the last name, but only a tiny amount that passed. We were both very much in agreement about it all. The only issue we had was with Felix's parents after the baby was born—they were concerned it would be difficult for Leon to have my last name.

—Elyse Truex, mother of Leon Truex

I knew my dad would be a bit upset but that wasn't difficult.

—Martin Bush, father of Remi and Aida Oke

Kudos!

If you're the mother, you may have to deal with people telling you and your partner how amazing and brilliant *he* is. Society still thinks that men are making the ultimate sacrifice by not passing on their last name, so they will get a lot of credit for this. It's not your partner's fault, but it might be a source of bemusement or irritation for you both.

Redressing societal imbalance

Passing on the mother's last name is a good way to redress the overall imbalance of baby last name distribution in the world. As Molly Caro, whose daughter has her last name, said in her popular essay on this topic on *The Hairpin* in 2014:

> *My hope: I want a pro-choice situation for last names. Instead of a given, how about a conversation between parents? Maybe someone wants a cohesive family name; maybe someone wants to honor a great-grandmother or grandfather; maybe someone wants to shed a last name and join a new family; maybe someone wants to give their child four last names and let the child pick at eighteen years old. I don't know. Something. Anything. Just not a given.*
>
> *I like to imagine a day when [my daughter] is hanging upside down from a soccer goal with her friends. The air is crisp. The talk is spirited. Last names are varied. And each child can tell the story of why, but it also doesn't matter as much because the pendulum has finally landed at center.*

A perspective on loss and gain

If you discard or lose something, like your last name, it's natural to focus on the thing that is lost. But it can be more helpful in a situation such as this to focus on what you will gain.

In the past, when women changed their last names at marriage, they gained social status, they became adults, and they became more respected members of society (because of the social value placed on marriage). To become "Mrs Rodney Jones" was something to take pride in.

For heterosexual men in particular, who were raised with the notion that they will pass their last names on to their children, it might be challenging to accept the idea of "losing" your last name. But consider what you will gain.

You are gaining a foothold in the future of equality. You are gaining the respect of your partner and, whether your child is a daughter or a son, you are teaching them from the outset that women's stories matter too. You are rejecting the "Shakespearean bastard" myth that we still hold over children who don't have an obvious nominal link to their fathers. You are contributing to the wider conversation about gender equality if you decide to explain your decision to others as your child grows up. And you are forging ahead with what feels right for your family as a whole and as a team.

You may also be giving a great gift to your partner, something that may be more meaningful to her than passing on your last name would be to you. You are making a statement, with every single form you fill out for your child, that fairness matters. You know that, while not everyone will make the same choice, you are, in some way, helping balance the scales, and contributing to change in the world.

6

DISCUSSING THIS OPTION WITH YOUR PARTNER

We've had a lot of discussions about this. We both feel strongly that a child should have its mother's last name, rather than its father's. We're also keen to retain the other last name as a middle name. (Last name hyphenation would be too troublesome.)

—David Laurence, in a relationship

It's something we have talked about for many years. We would often joke about it and find weird ways of combining our last names. There was not an obvious combination that worked, otherwise we might have used that for our child (our favorites were Fernandler and Wheelnandes).

I briefly considered changing my name after marriage but decided it was not something I wanted to do, and David was also of the opinion that I should keep my own name.

—Sophie Fernandes, mother of "Roo" Fernandes

[We talked about giving the baby my last name] maybe a few weeks before the birth. It may have come up years earlier though. Neither of us wanted to hurt the other's feelings. Philosophically I felt our first kid should have my name and my partner agreed/agrees. But it was probably a little scary for both of us to follow through. In the end I think he felt happy to be championing a "minority cause". I think I felt more uncomfortable than him initially.

—Linda Roberts, mother of Lev and Zadie Roberts

[We discussed this before] we decided to have children and then during the pregnancy. He re-affirmed the decision I had made to use my last name when we found out I was pregnant.

—Elyse Truex, mother of Leon Truex

Sometimes we'd talk about if we gave the child my last name what people would think ... Because all the women I know who kept their names if married or not, gave their child the partner's name. I started to feel weird about not having any role models, because I like being a front runner or an independent person but I also like knowing my research about what to expect ... So we'd have these kind of "what if" conversations ... Between ourselves, we decided on a handful of first names, some "maybe" names and then whatever name suited the baby, we'd settle on the last name.

—Amelia Chappelow, mother of Felix Chappelow

The decision was made when we got married six years before baby was born.

—Mark Kaneko, father of Ayaka Kaneko

It was an easy decision. He agreed that she would have my last name—we both feel it is a terrible injustice that women's histories are erased through marriage and that it's a given that men's names will prevail.

—Ada Conroy, mother of Pippa Conroy

Before we thought we would even have babies we discussed, agreed, and knew that a then-hypothetical baby would have [my partner's] family name.

—Martin Bush, father of Remi and Aida Oke

[We discussed] my last name [as an option]. My husband's name on its own was never an option.

—Kate Hegarty, mother of Theodore and Percival Hegarty-Bowen

I put forward the idea of using my last name and would do so again if we have another child.

—Megan Parker, mother of Iris O'Neill

We've talked all about the full name of our child if they are a girl, and it includes my last name as their proper last name, and his last name used as a sort of middle name, a nod to his family, and a way to make my parents not die of ethnic shame that their daughter is breaking her husband's balls.

—Sum Ambepitiya, married

I would have considered my ex-partner's last name if he'd pushed it, but he didn't.

—Vu Ngoc Hiep Huynh, mother of Noah Huynh

We sure have [discussed this option]! I believe in the principle that I get to name any and all things that come out of my vagina, so really I want any child of mine to have my last name, and they can have their father's last name as a

middle name (as I do) and then hyphenate or blend it when they are older. Chad wants to have a blended last name, but that seems like the kind of compromise that results in no one being entirely happy with the result. My last name has history and meaning and, as a history nut, those things are important to me. Obviously Chad probably feels the same way, but I basically think he should suck it up and take one for team feminism. Men have had naming rights over children and wives in Western cultures for long enough, and women have had to give up their identities for centuries, it's about time men sucked it up for a few generations and accepted that their children won't have the same name as them.

—Zora Sanders, married

I expressed my preference for a hyphenated, double-barrel, or blended last name. My partner said, in rebuttal, that "If it comes out of my vagina then I get to name it, and it will have my last name." I can't really argue with that.

—Chad Parkhill, married

He would have liked to have a child with his last name.

—Lucy Filor, mother of Maggie Filor

We were both happy to use either name, though I think I was slightly more attached to my last name.

—Judy Waugh, mother of Amelia and Fiona Waugh

I wanted them to have my last name since I was giving birth, but we wanted her [my partner's] name there too. We agreed the children could make changes themselves, as one has.

—Rebecca Harris, mother of Ella Harris and Noah Rundell-Harris

---

My wife never wanted to change her family name. She felt strongly connected to her family. I wanted my children to share this and felt no connection to my own family name so I suggested I change mine. Initially I had wanted to hyphenate our names but my partner didn't want this.

—Mark Kaneko, father of Ayaka Kaneko

I considered my last name, but we ruled it out early on for fairness reasons.

—Clare Rae, mother of Fox Palmerae

7

DIFFICULTIES (OR LACK OF) RESULTING FROM THIS CHOICE

Choosing a first name actually was more difficult as my (ex-)partner was extremely picky. [There have been no difficulties with the last name], as my son and I share the same last name and I have 100 per cent custody.

—Vu Ngoc Hiep Huynh, mother of Noah Huynh

Maybe [difficulties] will [come] later? He's only two! My husband a few times has been called Mr Chappelow and myself Mrs instead of Ms ... But that's about it! I thought there would be more stories!

—Amelia Chappelow, mother of Felix Chappelow

[We've just had "the usual" difficulties]. People assume we've all taken my partner's name. I don't know if he's been called Mr

Roberts yet, but that will be funny when it happens. I get called Mrs Roberts all the time when I take the kids to the doctor and things like that, though I've never changed my name or identified as a Mrs.

—Linda Roberts, mother of Lev and Zadie Roberts

This surprised me, but no friends, family, school or government official has ever asked why [my daughter] doesn't have her father's last name, and Inez has never questioned it.

—Daine Singer, mother of Inez Singer

As yet [we've had no difficulties] but she is only seven months old. I have been asked on a few occasions why her last name isn't the same as either mine or her father's (her certificate is pinned to the refrigerator) and I've explained the reasoning. If I start to run into regular trouble down the track, I'll look into changing my last name officially to match hers.

—Renae Whale, mother of Avery Carolan

Sometimes people call my partner Mr Conroy, but that's not a problem. He'll answer to that.

—Ada Conroy, mother of Pippa Conroy

[I get occasional] sideways glances because there is no father's name on my daughter's birth certificate. I'm a high school teacher and during pregnancy and after some of my students went from calling me Miss or Ms Baker to Mrs Baker! I guess they just assumed that baby=married.

—Sarah Baker, mother of June Baker

Some of Maggie's father's family have sent Maggie cards titled "Maggie Taylor" [her father's last name].

—Lucy Filor, mother of Maggie Filor

People assume I'm married and took my partner's last name when they hear Leon's and my last name is Truex. Forms for children aren't really set up to favor our arrangement. Leon is too young to have had any issues yet. Personally, having my mother's last name rather my father's [I find] that forms often ask for your mother's maiden name but not your father's (my parents both changed their last name when they married). I'm hoping there will be no issue with the choice we made, and I'm quite happy to correct anyone who is mistaken about our family relationship. [My partner] Felix's mother did make a fuss when she first met our son on the day I had given birth, she looked shocked that Scholz wasn't Leon's last name and acted very worried that he would struggle in life with Truex as his last name. The dagger eyes I gave her in my post-birth haze I think told her quietly to shut the fuck up and deal with the choice we had made.

—Elyse Truex, mother of Leon Truex

[I anticipate] having to explain why the child was given their mother's last name and not their father's.

—Andrea Williams, in a relationship

I had a different last name to my father. It was just awkward—it wouldn't be a problem now.

—Samone Bos, mother of Saffron and Jasper Bos

It was tricky and I still have to explain why I chose to take my wife's last name as I clearly do not look Japanese. There were some hurdles initially changing my name in my British passport.

—Mark Kaneko, father of Ayaka Kaneko

8

REGRETS (OR LACK OF) ARISING FROM THIS CHOICE

No *[regrets]. Never. I don't wish to disrespect the "It's just easier" brigade, maybe I live in a bubble, but not once in nearly ten years has there been a single incidence of confusion/uncertainty/ID required etc.*

—Martin Bush, father of Remi and Aida Oke

I don't [have any regrets], as it has made things very simple since the separation.

—Vu Ngoc Hiep Huynh, mother of Noah Huynh

No, I haven't [had any regrets]. I think [my partner's] okay with it.

—Lucy Filor, mother of Maggie Filor

We made this decision about six months into the pregnancy, and with not long to go until the birth it's something we've shared with family and friends and a decision we feel very comfortable with.

—Sophie Fernandes, mother of "Roo" Fernandes

I found it remarkably easy for my daughter to take my name, and am always surprised that other women don't consider it, or don't consider double-barreled names, even when they make many other feminist choices in their personal lives. I've seen many reasons given, such as difficulty at school, confusion on forms, tradition etc. but in practice haven't found those to have been any problem at all.

—Daine Singer, mother of Inez Singer

Sometimes I feel bad for my partner. I thought the second [child] would have his name, but he didn't want them to have two different names, so they both have mine.

—Linda Roberts, mother of Lev and Zadie Roberts

III

OPTION 3: HYPHENATED OR UNHYPHENATED DOUBLE-BARRELED LAST NAME

There is no easy way to say this, but no other last name form inspires as much hatred as the double-barreled last name. Some people loathe it, saying it's too long or too complicated or too difficult to spell, as well as: 'But what will the next generation do when they have kids'?! But for other couples, it's the perfect solution.

Whether you use a hyphen to join the names, or decide to use your two last names as separate words (think *Helena Bonham Carter* or *Sacha Baron Cohen*), this option feels truly equitable. The hyphenated last name even *looks* like balance scales.

We wanted both our families acknowledged in the naming.

Maybe being older parents we were more attached to names we'd happily lived with for so long.

—Joanne Haywood, mother of Freyja and Aubrey Haywood-Mace

I was willing to give up the hyphenated last name after my father gave my daughter her Chinese middle name. Knowing that on her birth certificate she would always have a Chinese name comforted me, and I was actually quite happy to leave the final decision to my husband. I didn't push him, and he went with the hyphenated name in the end. He may not have finalized that decision till I went into labor, in fact.

—Diane Tam, mother of Jude and Lou Tarricone-Tam

It was one of the factors that led to us getting married and changing our name. We both wanted to share our name with our hypothetical child, which led us to realize we wanted to share a name with each other, which led us to realize that we wanted to be married.

—Lefa Singleton Norton, mother of Avery Singleton Norton

I chose the hyphenated version. I liked how it sounded, I also liked that it is to me an indication that we are feminists [and we] thought it over. I sometimes wish I had just given [the children] my last name—their names are quite long.

—Kate Hegarty, mother of Theodore and Percival Hegarty-Bowen

Liked the sound and it included both our names.

—Nicholas Brody, father of Arlo and Mabel Brody-Wall

It was really important to me that the children had a hyphenated name as we are a same-sex couple. I felt this would protect against people perceiving the children as having a "real" mother if they just carried one name. If they carried both our last names, in my mind, it meant schools etc. would not know who was the biological mother and hopefully treat us equally as parents. Jo wasn't worried about this so I drove the conversation. I have had a male partner in the past and we had discussed children and, had we had them, they would've had a hyphenated last name of both our names, or just my last name, as I would never have agreed to follow the patriarchal "rule" of giving the children only the father's name.

—Pia Cerveri, mother of Ori and Arlo Cerveri-Ward

For a long time, our daughter was only going to have Smith as her last name and Fenech as her middle name. After much thought, we decided that Fenech-Smith did sound fine. It wasn't too big! I guess there are some benefits to having a simple last name such as Smith. I suggested [Fenech-Smith] to [my partner] Jake and initially he was against it. Purely because he wasn't keen on double-barreled last names. One day he just announced to some friends who were visiting that our baby would have Fenech-Smith as its last name. It took me by surprise, but I was really happy. So was my family.

—Mary-Jane Fenech, mother of Iris Fenech-Smith

We knew that starting our own family, we could do things how we wanted. So our boys are part of both of us, and the last names worked the same way.

—Nikki Brown, mother of Finn and Leo Larsen-Brown

[It was a] conversation when [we were] filling in forms to register the birth of the first child. I put Haynes as the last name; my husband said, "Don't you want Elliott as well?" So we used both.

—Jeanette Elliott, mother of Elizabeth, Miriam and Suzannah Elliott Haynes

---

[My ex] was happy for them to be Devenys. I chose to hyphenate them to Deveny-Borg. Growing up, it always seemed so strange kids all having their father's name. So it still seemed strange the thought of them having just mine. Hyphenated has been perfect. If my current partner and I had a baby, the name would be hyphenated and we would toss a coin to see whose name went first.

—Catherine Deveny, mother of Dom, Hugo and Charlie Deveny-Borg

---

It is important for me to think about passing on the Howie name [my mother's last name]. Also, my partner might also want to pass on their family name—either their mother's or father's. I am not opposed to hyphenating last names, but sometimes hyphenated names can get a bit messy—in terms of how the name sounds. I think if I was to hyphenate the child's name, I would prefer to use my partner's mother's name, because I would like to support matriarchal practices and processes.

—Tace Kelly, in a relationship

I would rather not give my child a hyphenated name as I don't enjoy mine being hyphenated. I think it's nice for both sides of the family to represented in the name somehow!

—Eliza-Jane Henry-Jones, married

I don't understand why a few of my friends are so against hyphenated names! They're fine, I don't get what the problem is! Seems like a good way of acknowledging both parents.

—Christina Cox, in a relationship

I wanted my kids to identify with both parents' own identities, and if, when they are older, they want to change their names that's their right to do so.

—Rachel Gadsden, mother of Samuel and Molly Gadsden-Chadd

We felt it was important to include both of our names, and that the children have the same names, to show the world that they are our children together and that they are siblings. We felt it was important given that we are a same-sex couple.

—Lisa Wise, mother of Gaby, Beth and Ted Crossley-Wise

Part of my insistence on my own last name for myself and my son is that I am a stepmother. I adore my stepsons and would walk over hot coals for them, but a stepparent lacks power in really significant ways, which can put huge strain on relationships. This was one way of asserting that I matter, and that I choose a certain path for my own son that I can't for the other children in my care.

—Hilary Milton, mother of Clancy Milton Woolf

9

ISSUES TO CONSIDER WITH THIS OPTION

Length

"Will there be enough boxes on the form?" is a reasonable concern. Some people are more willing than others to deal with the possible inconvenience that a longer name might bring. But long last names are more common than they may seem, and, increasingly, it is the forms themselves that are changing to accommodate them. Web designers are also much more mindful these days of cultural variations when building online forms, and creating more flexibility to accommodate different alphabetical characters, as well as longer names.

We discussed during the pregnancy [that I wanted to hyphenate our names for various reasons, and wondered:] would the children know they were part Chinese otherwise, in a dominant white and American culture?) He was against making their last names so long. We joked about smushing the names together into Tamicone.

—Diane Tam, mother of Jude and Lou Tarricone-Tam

Our last names are both long and difficult so we did not hyphenate, but I'd have considered this otherwise.

—Eva Ruggiero, mother of Harper and Ani Johnson

Hyphenated names are a bit ridiculous and not fun for the child to write on their schoolwork, but to each their own.

—Vu Ngoc Hiep Huynh, mother of Noah Huynh

It was more important for my partner's mother for our children to have both names, so hyphenated was an easy choice. We now reflect that our children's last names are too long and it's been hard for them to write it all when younger. They shorten it and refer to themselves as ConMacs.

—Melissa Connor, mother of Persephone and Adonis Connor-Macintyre

I think names are important and not important all at once! For me, it was very important to bestow upon my children the most fair and equal name that represented their parentage and connection to them. At the same time, hyphenated last names are clumsy and I know a lot of adults who revert to using only one part of their hyphenated name. If my children chose to do this, or change any part of their first or last names then I would be supportive of that, it's just that I wanted to start them off on a level playing field.

—Pia Cerveri, mother of Ori and Arlo Cerveri-Ward

Whose name will go first?

This decision is usually based on sound and rhythm.

We agreed early on that hyphenating works well and sounds best with my name first (i.e. Brody-Wall).

—Nicholas Brody, father of Arlo and Mabel Brody-Wall

Brown-Larsen sounded a bit weird, so it was an easy choice. [We wondered whether it] would it be hard for them to remember or write? We weren't worried about what others thought.

—Nikki Brown, mother of Finn and Leo Larsen-Brown

Aesthetics and euphony

A similar concern—how do the names sound together?

I guess the hyphenating worked well for us because they kind of sound good together. Someone told me that it's more traditional to, when hyphenating, have the male's name second. I mean that's insane, it should be what's easier and better to say. I guess there's heaps of names that sound ridiculous when hyphenated so I guess this solution is not for everyone but it worked for us.

—Nicholas Brody, father of Arlo and Mabel Brody-Wall

Confusion

If you don't use a hyphen to connect the last names (i.e. like Helena Bonham Carter or Sacha Baron Cohen) there might be a risk that one of the names will drop off. You might have to be really determined to ensure your child is known by both the names, as some people may think the first last name is a middle name, instead of part of the last name.

We don't use a hyphen, but the Medicare card and some other documents have a hyphen inserted.

—Jeanette Elliott, mother of Elizabeth, Miriam and Suzannah Elliott Haynes

Too fancy?

Some couples report that the hyphenated last name sounds too fancy or "posh" for their liking, as if the baby belongs to the English upper class. It's common enough for "ordinary" people to do it in many places around the world, but perhaps it's a consideration depending on where you live.

Other couples joke that connecting their last names together will make their kid's name sound like a law firm. This is pretty silly really, but worth mentioning as it's another one of the biases against hyphenation.

The next generation

This is a big question for a lot of people. What will your children do when they grow up and have their own kids?

Katie Roiphe, in an article for *Slate* in 2004, went as far as to say that hyphens are not only aesthetically disastrous, but socially irresponsible:

> *What happens when Julian Hesser-Friend marries Tessa Rosenfeld-Cassidy? Their grandchildren could end up with great, long, loopy strings of names, their signatures spilling off the blanks of any form.*

To me, that opinion shows a lack of imagination. Obviously, not everyone is inclined towards this option, and yes, your children *will* have to make their own decisions later on (just like, let's not forget, they will have to make *all* their own adult decisions later on), but the honest truth is that for many couples, hyphenated last names are an excellent solution.

My advice is to trust that the world is changing fast and your kids will manage. So do what feels best for you as a couple, now.

The parents who choose this option give their kids credit that they'll be able to work things out when the time comes—they might even have more motivation to raise their children as independent thinkers who will possess the ability to solve this last name dilemma for themselves when the time comes.

Well, figuring out how you pass on an already hyphenated last name and then also include the last name of a partner is tricky. My feeling is we would definitely pass on Twyford, and then perhaps drop the Moore (sorry Dad) and perhaps do a merge with my partner's last name, which is Mullane. So the kid would be Twyford-Mullane. Which you know, really does work and pays tribute to both—although the gender ordering has been changed somewhat. Yes, the double-barreled generation have it tough.

—Sam Twyford-Moore, married

10

DISCUSSING THIS OPTION WITH YOUR PARTNER

We discussed it prior to conception but we have also been together since we were twenty-one and married at twenty-six. When we married we decided that neither of us would change our name. During pregnancy we nicknamed our fetus "Hegbo" but I was adamant that our baby would have my last name and my husband agreed, but also said he did like the hyphenated version. To be honest I sort of chickened out of giving just my name—which is actually ludicrous. However, I do also like Hegarty-Bowen.

—Kate Hegarty, mother of Theodore and Percival Hegarty-Bowen

We discussed [it] during the pregnancy. I wanted just Connor, but as my partner's mother was dying it was important to her to have Macintytre in our daughter's last name. So, for her, we decided to hyphenate.

—Melissa Connor, mother of Persephone and Adonis Connor-Macintyre

---

It was hard for me to broach wanting my partner to take on my name as I felt it was asking him to put a target on his back. His friends and family would all react and ask questions, and I felt like it fed into a narrative about him being "made" to do it. He was happy to make the name change, but felt very self-conscious about it and took a long time to make it publicly known that he had changed his name.

—Lefa Singleton Norton, mother of Avery Singleton Norton

It was never anything personal. It was always more to do with whether having a double-barreled last name would be annoying for our daughter. I always wanted her to have Smith in her name (many people couldn't understand why I wouldn't just give her my last name alone). However, it was important to me for Iris to have her father's name, even if it is such a common name.

—Mary-Jane Fenech, mother of Iris Fenech-Smith

[There is the] difficulty of our last names being a little unwieldy hyphenated.

—Luke Horton, in a relationship

Our last names would sound so weird together.

—Darcey Bloom, in a relationship

I think we both just felt really clear that we wanted our daughter to have our own last name, and neither of us was willing to give it up, so we ended up choosing a hyphenated last name, which felt like a compromise at the time. But now I love that she has both of our names (though it's pretty damn long) and I have become a fan of hyphenated last names. I love seeing the odd combos, and that it feels like a beautiful collaboration. Our conversations around this topic were tense at times—I think that Kalu may have felt frustrated that I wasn't happy for Elvie to take his last name, like nearly all of the other babies we know. I still feel surprised by how few mothers I know care about their child taking their last name in one way or another. I think I was a bit calmer, because I never really expected to convince him that our baby should take my name only, so settling on the hyphenated name was less of a surprise or disappointment for me.

—Jane Winning, mother of Elva Ribush-Winning

I actually wanted Freyja to be Haywood rather than have both our names. I felt that taking the mother's name more accurately reflects the circumstances of our birth—we are conceived and grown within, and then birthed from, and often fed by our mother's bodies after all. However, I could easily relate to my partner wanting his children to carry his name too, and we agreed on a hyphenation even though I do find it a bit clunky. I think my desire for my children to carry my name was a bit confronting for him, but in fact it was probably harder for me to compromise, as I do feel strongly that women's history has been so ignored by patrilineal descent.

—Joanne Haywood, mother of Freyja and Aubrey Haywood-Mace

One sticking point was that my husband has two sons from his first marriage who have his last name and he wanted our baby to have the same name to consolidate their bond. I have half- and step-siblings with completely different names to mine and I consider them family, so that didn't fly with me.

—Hilary Milton, mother of Clancy Milton Woolf

The hyphenated silly business didn't stand a chance. One child really doesn't like the [last name] he has, and would prefer mine ... I told him he can change it when he is older.

—Emily Goode, mother of Arlo, Bertrand and Lyle Godfrey

[We considered] hyphen[ation] ... but [it was] too long and cumbersome.

—Renee Mills, mother of Ari and Elvie Mahoney

Our hyphenated names would have sounded ridiculous!

—Jessica Worrall, mother of Elise Worrall

[We discussed] keeping our own last names and double-barreling [our son's].

—Lefa Singleton Norton, mother of Avery Singleton Norton

We considered double-barreled but Turner-Luce didn't really work! ('Turn her loose?')

—Jo Turner, mother of Toby, Phoebe and Max Luce

The two options for me were only my name or hyphenating both our names.

—Joanne Haywood, mother of Freyja and Aubrey Haywood-Mace

We tried hyphenating and combining our names, but found the results pretty unwieldy, and chose to go for something straightforward.

—Jessica Friedmann, mother of Owen Baylis

We did consider just "Chadd". Peer pressure was coming in to avoid the double-barrel last name; however, I didn't see it would be a problem. A name is a name and people need to respect it.

—Rachel Gadsden, mother of Samuel and Molly Gadsden-Chadd.

We considered mine or his. I am not a fan of hyphenated last names, because it solves the problem for us, but creates a problem for the kid when it's their turn to make this decision. Also, in the United Kingdom they are considered "posh" and would seem silly to them. We didn't consider making a new name, because neither of us intended to change our last name we were born with—we both believe it is something we carry through life and that marriage doesn't give us a new identity.

—Ellen Angus, mother of Georgina Mant

[We considered] Fisk-Hoang. She may still be renamed this if [my partner Joseph and I] are allowed to marry.

—Anthony Fisk, father of Celeste Fisk

I think the harder part [of the discussion] was on me (though I don't know if he'd confirm this) because of loss of identity that is racial and cultural, based on our patriarchal assumption to name children by the father's family.

—Diane Tam, mother of Jude and Lou Tarricone-Tam

I was the one giving birth and I felt strongly that they should have my last name, but I wanted my partner's name in there too, so made it a middle name. We agreed the children could make changes themselves, as one has.

—Helen Ross, mother of Zoe Ross and Flynn Harding-Ross

11

DIFFICULTIES (OR LACK OF) RESULTING FROM THIS CHOICE

We have had] no real difficulties. Teachers choose to call the kids usually just Tam—folks don't know what to do with the hyphen, and the kids appear more Asian than white. But no really funny situations. I do think it makes taking the kids around and out of the country a little easier on both parents, because they both bear our actual last names, and it doesn't appear that a white guy is kidnapping two Asian kids if he's traveling by himself with them.

—Diane Tam, mother of Jude and Lou Tarricone-Tam

People think that [my partner's and my] names are also hyphenated. We don't mind.

—Lisa Wise, mother of Gaby, Beth and Ted Crossley-Wise

If we drop my father's last name—would he take it personally?

—Sam Twyford-Moore, married

People hate the length!

—Melissa Connor, mother of Persephone and Adonis Connor-Macintyre

---

Some people have assumed the last name is just Wall, my wife's last name, rather than Brody-Wall, probably because it's last. It didn't bother me.

—Nicholas Brody, father of Arlo and Mabel Brody-Wall

[We've had no] difficulties so far; officially and legally the kids are "Gadsen-Chadd" but they are known as Chadd until they are a bit older and can understand.

—Rachel Gadsden, mother of Samuel and Molly Gadsden-Chadd.

My son wanted to hyphenate the last names, so we changed his

name last year. He is eleven. Now he and his sister have different last names but it doesn't bother anyone.

—Helen Ross, mother of Zoe Ross and Flynn Harding-Ross

Some [people] didn't see why it meant so much to me. Others felt we'd created a rod for our son's back—what are his kids supposed to do—have four last names? We think that's for him to negotiate with his partner in time.

—Hilary Milton, mother of Clancy Milton Woolf

The main difficulty for us is that my partner already has a hyphenated last name. So do we take one or both of the names from her last name and hyphenate them with mine, or do we create a new name? We wouldn't want to make life hell for the child!

—Jen Clark, in a relationship

I don't think issues arise in this day and age. It's common now compared to twenty years ago.

—Rachel Gadsden, mother of Samuel and Molly Gadsden-Chadd

I'm from a family of multiple marriages and multiple last names and the world has never come to an end.

—Hilary Milton, mother of Clancy Milton Woolf

[We have had] absolutely no [difficulties]. Also, in Indonesia where we were living for nearly four years, often boys have their father's last name and girls have their mother's. No big deal. And women very rarely change their name upon marriage. Australia is still so rigid about this stuff.

—Kate Hegarty, mother of Theodore and Percival Hegarty-Bowen

[We have had no difficulties] at all. People get very uptight about this idea, but names have changed throughout the ages for all sorts of reasons. I just don't think it matters to have different names within one family, and when people worry about it they're often appearing to worry about children not having the father's last name, which is an archaic patriarchal concept.

—Pia Cerveri, mother of Ori and Arlo Cerveri-Ward

Some friends who met my children first assumed my last name was the same as theirs.

—Jeanette Elliott, mother of Elizabeth, Miriam and Suzannah Elliott Haynes

---

[My] husband was offended that I was bucking the trend, and his family's opinion weighed heavily on his shoulders. My family fully supported any decision I was to make, as it was my business. At times it still is a sore point for hubby and his family. But not for me, or the kids. We're all good with it, especially when traveling.

—Rachel Gadsden, mother of Samuel and Molly Gadsden-Chadd

The only difficult thing we thought may have been the reactions of his family—who actually do drop the hyphen and just say Bowen!

—Kate Hegarty, mother of Theodore and Percival Hegarty-Bowen

12

REGRETS (OR LACK OF) ARISING FROM THIS CHOICE

No [regrets]! Well, his brother did make a crack about how long my daughter's name was. But not real regret, that I know of.

—Diane Tam, mother of Jude and Lou Tarricone-Tam

I haven't [had any regrets]. I'm not 100 per cent sure about my partner—he hasn't said anything, but I haven't asked him.

—Jane Winning, mother of Elva Ribush-Winning

It feels like the best choice we could have made given our own feelings, but I sometimes feel like we've burdened him with an over-complicated name.

—Lefa Singleton Norton, mother of Avery Singleton Norton

Sometimes [I've had regrets], as it is hard for the kids to write. People often think their first name is Connor and last name Macintyre. There can be impatience in people wanting to write both last names. The kids say they feel cool having a unique name.

—Melissa Connor, mother of Persephone and Adonis Connor-Macintyre

Sometimes I wish I chose only my name as my kids' names are quite long! Plus, [there is] the feminist statement of having just my name. But I think a hyphenated name is also a statement.

—Kate Hegarty, mother of Theodore and Percival Hegarty-Bowen

I haven't [had any regrets]. I don't know about my partner but I'd be surprised if she had regrets.

—Pia Cerveri, mother of Ori and Arlo Cerveri-Ward

IV

OPTION 4: A BLEND OF BOTH

I mentioned earlier in the book that I genuinely thought this sounded like a joke the first time I heard of it. But I gradually warmed to it when it became clear that both my partner and I were reluctant to give up our last names entirely, and as you know, this is the last-name option we ultimately used for our children.

We love it, and this book wouldn't exist if I hadn't personally experienced the liberation and joyfulness that has come from finding an alternative last name option that works for us.

We were already known as "The Palmeraes" to our friends as a couple, so it seemed natural to give our baby our blended name. We had a few discussions over whether it sounded too ridicu-

lous, but eventually decided it was the right, and fair, thing to do.

—Clare Rae, mother of Fox Palmerae

We thought it would be clever and cutting edge, since we live in the inner-suburbs of our city, and we not only have to buy all the latest gear for our child (SUV pram, razor scooter, etc.), we also have to set ourselves apart from the throngs. We felt the name of our child (Dean is ungendered, by the way) was the way to really disrupt the norm.

—Artemis Balnave, mother of Dean Balrez

13

ISSUES TO CONSIDER WITH THIS OPTION

Splitting and blending

This can be tricky, and you will soon discover that some last name couplings were just never meant to be. But even if both names can be easily split in half, you will still need to ask yourselves what order they should go in, and what combination sounds best.

Culture clash

Some last name integrations sound very odd together, especially if they originate from two very different linguistic heritages. You may need to ask yourself: does it sound too culturally confusing or strange?

On the other hand, you might have two last names that have a similar cultural providence that, when spliced together, "sound" like they belong to another culture entirely. This might be appealing to you, or it might not!

My partner is very open-minded but I am conscious of having both our heritages evident in the name without creating a name that sounds "wrong".

—Sushani Kandhan, married

My partner's name is Strong but I don't think we could subject a person to living with the name Strongcox or Strong-Cox or whatever. As much as I would love that because it's hilarious, it seems cruel to name someone with your own funny portmanteau that you made up if your name is Cox.

—Christina Cox, in a relationship

What will the neighbors think?

Some people just can't get their heads around this solution. Why take half of each name, and thus sever connections to both? I can only speak from my perspective here: we don't feel like we're severing anything; rather, to us it feels that we're honoring both branches of the family tree.

A long line of abuelas would be horrified if their grandchild didn't carry the Alvarez legacy.

—Artemis Balnave, mother of Dean Balrez

Family unity

With this option, unless you and your partner also change your names, you will have three different last names, so you might feel some anxiety as to how society will identify you as a family. This comes back to your core values about what makes a family. What are the things that are important to you? Are people smart enough to know you're a family despite your having different last names? Can you deal with some people being confused, and having to explain it sometimes? Which brings me to:

You might find yourself explaining it

One of the loveliest consequences about any of these last name choices, but especially the more unusual ones, is that people might be curious enough to ask you where it came from, and you'll get to tell the story. And your kids will get to tell it too. "It's a combination of both my parents' names" is a beautiful answer to the question "Where does your last name come from?" The sense of family "unity" you might have feared losing may actually be created by emphasizing the parental equality that led to this naming decision.

We both felt it was important to give our son part of each of our names. I would've preferred our kids to have my last name, but it's not fair to my partner, so we created a new name with both our names in it.

—Clare Rae, mother of Fox Palmerae

The English language

English is a living and breathing organism that we make work for us every day. Times change, and so do language conventions and words. They have been changing for centuries, and will continue to change. As a working editor, I reassure myself often with this knowledge, knowing that language and style is constantly changing and being updated. Lots of words used to be two, but over time have become one. Words that used to have hyphens or spaces—like ice-cream, or thank you—are now frequently joined together. The world of language is moving forward, and fast.

This is not to say that if you're traditionally minded you are behind the times or wrong. It's just that our world can (or should be able to) accommodate conservative and progressive choices equally, depending on what type of person you are. And if you are the sort of person who looks to the future rather than the past, be assured that the language will be malleable enough to come along with you.

Finally, a reminder: you might play it safe and stick with something conventional for your kids, but in all likelihood they will be the ones to change things up when they have kids.

14

DISCUSSING THIS OPTION WITH YOUR PARTNER

The more I discuss this with my boyfriend, the more I'm coming around to the blended last name solution. He is Hart and I am Stefanovic. He likes blended last names and suggested Hartovic, though I think it's a bit strange, as it is an ethnic mash-up. It looks like a Yugoslavian name, though it isn't. I wanted alternating names (for example, boys Stefanovic; girls Hart). I don't care if siblings have the same last name or not. But the more I think about Hartovic, I kind of like it. Partly because it would annoy both our families, and start something new.

—Sofija Stefanovic, in a relationship

As a feminist it became hard to justify giving my children my father's name as it's in some ways re-inscribing patriarchal naming rules.

—Clare Rae, mother of Fox Palmerae

[We discussed] a smush: instead of Tarricone-Tam, Tamicone; also, just Tarricone.

—Diane Tam, mother of Jude and Lou Tarricone-Tam

We thought briefly about a portmanteau but I would classify this more as a musing than a consideration. Now that my family have three different last names we've discussed inventing a last name for us all to go by, but it wouldn't be okay with [my ex-partner] Daniel's dad. We also don't really care that much.

—Anna Gottstein, mother of Daniel Archer

Sometime after she was born a friend started calling her Elvie Winbush—an amalgamation of our last names—and there is something about this that is really appealing to me. However, I think we still would have gone with a hyphenated name even if we'd thought of Winbush at the time.

—Jane Winning, mother of Elva Ribush-Winning

We tried to combine our last names, but nothing worked. Given I had already changed my first name, I didn't want to erase myself entirely, so we decided against one name for us all.

—Ada Conroy, mother of Pippa Conroy

We sometimes joked about creating a new last name by combining ours.

—Sarah McCallan, mother of Philippa and Benjamin Wallace

We considered no last name—like Prince—but that would prove troublesome for university admissions.

—Artemis Balnave, mother of Dean Balrez

I definitely wanted my children to have my last name. It was personal preference and political. I chose to hyphenate with their dad's name. We've told the boys they can drop a name, or whatever. They love their last name.

—Catherine Deveny, mother of Dom, Hugo and Charlie Deveny-Borg

15

DIFFICULTIES (OR LACK OF) RESULTING FROM THIS CHOICE

P*eople think they've spelled [our daughter's last name] wrong when they hear or see my partner's name. It's not too bad.*

—Clare Rae, mother of Fox Palmerae

I'm not sure yet, as Dean is still in early development stages, but I will defend [our choice] to the end.

—Artemis Balnave, mother of Dean Balrez

16

REGRETS (OR LACK OF) RESULTING FROM THIS CHOICE

No! *I love our baby's name and the connections it signifies.*

—Clare Rae, mother of Fox Palmerae

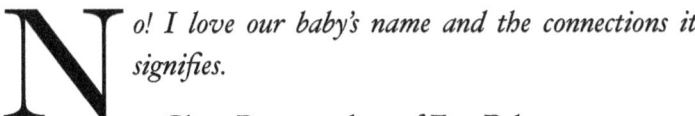

[I have never had regrets]. And so many of the mothers at the cafés I frequent commend me on my choice.

—Artemis Balnave, mother of Dean Balrez

V

OPTION 5: ALTERNATING LAST NAMES FOR SIBLINGS

Here is an option for couples who are pretty sure they'll have another child (or who already have one). Alternating the last names is a great way to share both names out across the family.

We both wanted to give our children our family name, so in the end we decided to alternate. Our daughter has my last name and her father's last name as a middle name; our next child will have his last name and my last name as a middle name. If we have a third, they will have my last name and his as a middle name. We did not want to hyphenate, so this was the decision we were most comfortable with.

—Erin Jeffers, mother of Eva Jeffers

We were unencumbered by any earlier issues, we just didn't support the patriarchal naming convention. We would have hyphenated but thought that it becomes cumbersome (especially over generations).

—Sandra Pitcher, mother of Tess Manwaring and Matilda Pitcher

17

ISSUES TO CONSIDER WITH THIS OPTION

Social expectations

Here we come back to social pressure. If one child has the father's last name and the other child has the mother's, will people think that the kids have different parents? How will schools cope? Making the family connection between siblings clear from the outset may help here. People who know you will know the kids are siblings, obviously, and for the wider social circle it's easy enough (and fascinating!) to explain the reason.

This is something you will either be concerned about, or not. The idea that people who are already in your life would gauge parentage through the last names alone seems a bit strange, though. When it comes to schools knowing which children are siblings, keep in mind that kids have different last names to each other for lots of reasons now. It doesn't take much to introduce you and your children to the teachers from the outset and help them make the family connection, if it's a real concern you might have in the future. Similarly, in doctor's offices or anywhere else it comes up, a simple sentence—"The kids have different last names because one has mine and one has my partner's"—isn't that difficult to explain.

When you make a conscious last name decision such as this, one that is based on core values, it's unlikely you will be concerned or overly irritated about having to explain it when it comes up. You might even enjoy it!

I have found the variety of last names at school and childcare more diverse than we could've imagined. However, we were surprised by how many friends toyed with options but in the end reverted to using [the father's] last name.

—Sandra Pitcher, mother of Tess Manwaring and Matilda Pitcher

---

I think I'm more interested in last names than my boyfriend (he wouldn't mind if I wanted to give the kids my last name, for example). I like the idea of alternating names, as this option honors both parents. As for what other people think? My boyfriend's family doesn't influence his decisions much (at least, not thus far), so I'm sure if they disapproved he wouldn't care.

I wonder if my family would hate it if we gave our kids a blended name, or alternating names? I think in some ways they

would, because they're not as innovative as I like to think with these things, but you never know, they may like it.

—Sofija Stefanovic, in a relationship

Family unity

It's hard to say if your children will feel separate from their siblings if they don't share a last name, because that will depend on the personality of your kids. Keep in mind that names can be changed down the track if strong feelings come up. Many siblings who share a last name feel disconnected and don't get along, while stepsiblings in blended families can feel close, even if they don't share a last name.

I come from a big family, and am a result of both my parents' second marriages. I have a lot of siblings with different names, it's never caused any issues, and I am actually closer to the siblings with a different last name.

—Clare Rae, mother of Fox Palmerae

Order

Whose name do you give to the first child? One way to solve this would be to toss a coin, or to pick a first name and then choose the last name that suits it best. You might then agree that a second child, regardless of gender, will get the other partner's last name. Or, are you in a relationship where you can go the gendered route, with boys taking their father's last name, and girls their mother's? (Or the other way round?) What if you only have boys, or girls? Would it matter to you if two daughters had two different last names, or two sons? These are all things to consider.

If you alternate last names by sex, for example by giving the father's last name if it's a boy and the mother's last name if it's a girl, this is still a gendered way to organize things. This might be just as unsatisfactory for couples who are trying to break gendered norms.

Tossing a coin, as ridiculous as it sounds, might be the best solution for couples in this situation.

There is always a possibility that, even if you plan on having two or more children, you will only have one. Will you still feel at peace with your decision if that happens?

18

DISCUSSING THIS OPTION WITH YOUR PARTNER

It was an ongoing discussion in the years before having our child.

—Erin Jeffers, mother of Eva Jeffers

We wanted to make sure that [our decision] wouldn't cause our children problems. We knew some of our parents wouldn't support our decision.

—Sandra Pitcher, mother of Tess Manwaring and Matilda Pitcher

19

DIFFICULTIES (OR LACK OF) RESULTING FROM THIS CHOICE

My family is very traditional when it comes to last names; however, my husband's family is not! On his mother's side (with the same last name), he has a half-sister, and on his father's side a half-brother. His father and half-brother have different last names. Also, his sister maintained her last name after marriage. My husband is from northern New South Wales [in Australia], and different family structures are quite common in that area, so he never had issues with family members all having different last names.

—Sophie Fernandes, mother of "Roo" Fernandes

I come from a blended family. People I call family have had different family names since I was ten. So no [difficulties].

—Martin Bush, father of Remi and Aida Oke

I come from a divorced family with a secondary step-family, so last names have never really held significance for me. They've always been easily interchangeable.

—Darcy Laughlin, mother of Emily Milne

My sister and I are from different fathers so it can be confusing at times, as we have different last names.

—Stephanie Brill, mother of Charlie Thompson

[We have had no] difficulties, it is just often assumed that both my daughter and I have my husband's last name. This is frustrating, especially when it comes from family who we have told more than once. People often tell us we are making life difficult for our children when they go to school, but we suspect our children will understand why they have their names, and what makes us a family, and will hopefully be able to educate others!

—Erin Jeffers, mother of Eva Jeffers.

[We have only had] one mild inconvenience traveling overseas in eight years!

—Sandra Pitcher, mother of Tess Manwaring and Matilda Pitcher

20

REGRETS (OR LACK OF) ARISING FROM THIS CHOICE

No [regrets]. We are very pleased we followed our initial plan—it has been easy, fair and makes sense to us. Our girls know they both have our last names, and they don't think it's strange or unusual. We are pleased with our decision, and our family have all accepted it without further issue or comment.

—Sandra Pitcher, mother of Tess Manwaring and Matilda Pitcher

VI

OPTION 6: A NEW LAST NAME

This is the unicorn of last name options, the giddy, phantasmagorical, do-we-dare option. It's a choice for couples who want to start their family anew, who feel the unity and strength of their own bond and look towards to the future rather than back the past. This solution can come up by surprise, and unexpectedly feel right for some families.

I couldn't stomach adhering to patriarchal traditions and consent to taking on my husband's last name. As much as I love hearing about husbands taking on their wives' last names, my life force is more driven by customizing and creating, and particularly as my last name isn't spectacular enough to insist on playing the feminist card, we decided to start a new lineage.

—Leah Emery, mother of Linka and Eartha Redzed

We shortened [my partner's] real name, and used that. I was happy as "Avanaki" shares a k with "Tulk". It may seem silly but I like the letters in "Avanaki" as they are similar to my total name.

—Jasmin Tulk, mother of Maryam Avanaki

I was adamant that I wanted my children to have matriarchal lineage in their names. But it wasn't easy to come up with something meaningful. I didn't want my father's name, nor my mother's family name so felt a little lost. Hyphenation didn't appeal but we wanted a nod to both sides of lineage. A new combined name felt completely right when we did some investigation and found both my maternal great-grandmothers happened to have the same prefix in their name. But later, we decided that for everyday use, having their own unique [last] names was more suitable [and this is what we have done].

—Cindy Renate, mother of Arminka Axelle and Elke Seraphine

I decided to pay homage to Avery's father by giving her his preferred nickname, "Yogi", as one of her two middle names, and giving her my middle name (which I use professionally as my last name) as her last name, "Carolan". The family significance is it is my great-grandmother's last name and is Irish. I felt that I could always change my last name officially by deed poll down the track if I wanted us to have matching last names.

—Renae Whale, mother of Avery Carolan

21

ISSUES TO CONSIDER WITH THIS OPTION

Unlimited choice

When you have unlimited choices, you can feel paralyzed. What sort of last name will you choose?

You could try choosing a name or word that means something to one of your families. For this, you can look back through your family history. Or perhaps it's the town where you met, or visited on your honeymoon? Is it one of your parents' birthplaces, or your father's middle name, or the name of your favorite flower? Only you can find the name that has the most significance and meaning to you both.

The last name I chose for our family, Redzed, is named after the Datsun 260Z "Redzed" car my father had when he met my mother. As legend has it, Dad had a brand-new Datsun, as did my mother when they met. They both thought the other was financially secure, but Dad owed a lot of money on his hot two-seater that wasn't able to accommodate children, and my mother was in debt to her dad. They were both paying off their Datsun debts for years to come! Plus the Redzed is an incredible and delightfully designed car.

—Leah Emery, mother of Linka and Eartha Redzed

A culturally suitable name

Depending on your situation, you may need to consider whether the last name you choose works in multiple languages.

Family unity

As with the blended last name and hyphenated last name choice, with this option you'll be dealing with three different last names in one family. Are you OK with this? Or will you, as parents, also change your last names to match your child's?

Family or social pressure

Your families might be confused and disappointed that you are not using their last names.

Family pressure is a real concern. My partner's mother is unlikely to understand if we both changed to a new last name.

—Joel Turner, in a relationship

I am very good at not worrying about family or cultural pressure and my fella and I have already had a good chat about this, so I don't anticipate any problems.

—Lara Murray, in a relationship

I'm hoping our mothers might be understanding that we've decided to create a new last name given that they both gave up their last names simply as a matter of course due to societal norms at the time. I don't know, though, because all of my brothers' children have been given the paternal last name!

—Nikki Lusk, mother of Zoë Summers

My parents would hate it [if we created a new last name]; my partner's parents and family might think it's weird. Society would make assumptions about who [a child's] parents were if [the parents] had a different last name. I would be worried my partner would be offended even though I wouldn't understand why.

—Agatha Morse, married

I don't think either side of our family have any particular expectations regarding names, and we're pretty good at nutting things out between us.

—Eliza-Jane Henry-Jones, married

It's unusual

That's true ... but new last names *are* becoming more common.

I think we're at a time when the tradition of naming is being re-examined, and I'm excited by the possibility of being part of changing the system by adopting a new naming tradition for my children that doesn't reflect an antiquated patriarchal hierarchy. I think it would be a very powerful symbol of gender equality to give our children a name that my husband and I have chosen together rather than one handed down through the father's line. I don't see it as causing any problems in people identifying us as a family (if people can only recognize a family by their name, it doesn't say much about the strength of that family unit), and I'm interested in the necessary society-wide conversation that this choice might contribute to.

—Nikki Lusk, mother of Zoë Summers

22

DISCUSSING THIS OPTION WITH YOUR PARTNER

We both have kind of difficult last names and it would be a shitty long hyphenated beast, so a new name might have to arise.

—Sommer Tothill, married

He didn't want our daughter to have his long name, but I didn't want her to have his Anglicized name as that means nothing—I preferred a shortened version of his name as the letters are similar to my name!

—Jasmin Tulk, mother of Maryam Avanaki

My husband's and my last name were never in contention. The continuation of my family name and obviously his are secure through many other family members, which would be a consideration of our families.

My husband is slightly more conservative, or perhaps logical and rational than me, so my more flamboyant suggestions were always vetoed. Now I'm thankful.

—Leah Emery, mother of Linka and Eartha Redzed

We did briefly toy with the idea of all of us changing our last names to something completely different and starting our own family name, but that idea kind of faded after a while [and we chose my last name].

—Cecilia Acevedo, mother of Silas Acevedo

I don't think we could have hyphenated or made up a name ... maybe we're not that creative.

—Amelia Chappelow, mother of Felix Chappelow

We thought about inventing a new last name for all of us, but that seemed silly in the end.

—Hop Dac Nguyen, father of Georgette Nguyen

23

DIFFICULTIES (OR LACK OF) RESULTING FROM THIS CHOICE

I often receive mail with incorrect spelling for the girls. Our first's birth certificate was spelled incorrectly. It's a name that we need to repeat and spell each time we use it. As it turns out, there happens to be a confectionery company based in Australia of the same name, which is quite nice as rather than being too alienated by their odd last name, the girls can find a biscuit with their name on it in most cafés and get a giggle out of it, in the same vein as me getting a kick out of filing my nails with emery boards or seeing an Emery medical trolley in hospital. Trivial yet endearing identity connections.

We often need to tell our story of why our family unit has three different last names, but it's a fun story to tell, and I don't mind telling it.

—Leah Emery, mother of Linka and Eartha Redzed

We recently had a scare at Tehran airport where we were questioned on why our daughter's name didn't match either of ours. It made me think about how we identify relations, and how we travel with children. I'll never go anywhere without her birth certificate and our marriage certificate again!

—Jasmin Tulk, mother of Maryam Avanaki

I anticipate having to answer a lot of questions from strangers or people we encounter as our children interact with the world, but I'm happy with that.

—Nikki Lusk, mother of Zoë Summers

24

REGRETS (OR LACK OF) ARISING FROM THIS CHOICE

In our situation there's no perfect last name. Without the luxury of a hundred years to ponder the best fitting option (and when beginning from scratch the possibilities are infinite, hence our difficulties!) I'm satisfied that it suits my requirements of honoring my father in my own way, and being able to custom-select a name that reflects our curious demeanor. My husband is easygoing and went with the flow, but it likely bothers him from time to time, as we need to repeat it and spell it every time.

—Leah Emery, mother of Linka and Eartha Redzed

OTHER NAMING OPTIONS TO HONOR YOUR FAMILIES

Now we've looked at the Six Last Name Options, let's talk about the other ways you can still represent or honor both families somewhere in the name if you decide not to carry on one of your last names.

People come up with lots of ways to do this. Middle names are a popular solution. Or else you could use the family name as a first name, or use the first names of parents, grandparents or other ancestors to honor your family heritage.

My husband's last name will be one of the middle names (Roo [has] a first name, middle name, husband's last name and my last name).

—Sophie Fernandes, mother of "Roo" Fernandes

We gave [my last name] to her as a second middle name. Partly to honor it, and partly so that on official documents my name is there as well.

—Kate Harris, mother of Georgette Nguyen

We had a boy first, so my kids have their dad's last name. I chose to give my firstborn my last name as his middle name, which gives me a sense of connection to my name. My partner chose our daughter's middle name and I was slightly disappointed he didn't keep with that tradition. However, he chose her middle name after my late mother, so I still have a strong connection, and it is prettier and easier to say and spell.

—Eva Ruggiero, mother of Harper and Ani Johnson

We used my partner's dad's first name as a middle name for my son.

—Linda Roberts, mother of Lev and Zadie Roberts

My son has my mother's maiden name—Miller—as his middle name. [There are] no men to carry that name on.

—Renee Mills, mother of Ari and Elvie Mahoney

My last name was given to Molly as her second middle name. If we were to have any other children, we would do the same for them.

—Kathleen Murphy, mother of Molly Wardle

My eldest son I named Andrew; my maiden name is Drew, but it had been used already in my family, so I named him Andrew.

—Tanya Greenbank, mother of Andrew, Samara and Morgan Golding, and Shiloh and Saige Greenbank

---

I gave my sons my maiden name (Wadsworth) as a middle name (so they have two middle names) and then Eldridge is their last name. I kind of figured it would help carry on my last name?

—Ann Wadsworth, mother of Daisy, Oscar and Ernest Eldridge

Both children have oblique references to my family in middle names. [My partner] suggested/asked if I wanted Bush as a middle name but no, you can't negotiate with patriarchy. Remi's middle name is the nickname of my father's father; Aida's middle name is a different spelling of my mother's mother.

—Martin Bush, father of Remi and Aida Oke

Rose is the middle name ([after my partner] Joseph's sister [who is the] egg donor).

—Anthony Fisk, father of Celeste Fisk

We did use [my partner's] paternal grandfather's name as his middle name so we still honored his family.

—Vu Ngoc Hiep Huynh, mother of Noah Huynh

Since we used my last name, we gave the kids middle names that related, and thus linked them to my partner's side of the family. For our first child the middle name was the name of his adored grandmother, and for our second child the middle name was the feminine version of my partner's name.

—Judy Waugh, mother of Amelia and Fiona Waugh

We considered Angus as a middle name, but I didn't like the sound of it enough to justify it. We are again considering it for baby number two (either as a first or middle name), but again I am not fond enough of the sound/look to justify it. (I just want it for political reasons, not for aesthetic reasons!) I'd rather honor other family names such as grandparents' first names.

—Ellen Angus, mother of Georgina Mant

Before I got married, my last name was my mother's last name. This was problematic growing up in [a] super-conservative regional [town] in the 1980s. Teachers were nosy jerks about it, particularly, and I felt a misplaced sense of shame. Now I'm really proud of the choices my mother made—refusing to marry or give me my father's last name—but growing up and having to explain myself was something I really resented. I honored her by giving my son a variation of her first name as his middle name (Julie to Julian).

—Samone Bos, mother of Saffron and Jasper Bos

We didn't honor the last name, but the children have names from that side of the family as their middle names.

—Rachel Cowling, mother of Fergus and Evie Cowling

Our daughter's first name is my grandmother's.

—Megan Parker, mother of Iris O'Neill

My son has my deceased brother's name as his middle name.

—Jane Fafeita, mother of Samuel and Aurora McCafferty

We used Kate's last name as one of Georgette's middle names. Her other middle name is Kate's maternal grandmother's first name.

—Hop Dac Nguyen, father of Georgette Nguyen

I've been thinking that if we have another baby and it's a boy, we could call it Lachlan. That's how people pronounce my last name in Australia (it's actually "Loff-Len") and I don't mind it as a first name ... it's pretty cute.

—Darcy Laughlin, mother of Emily Milne

My daughter has my grandmother's first name, so my side of the family has been included.

—Grace Imrie, mother of Lincoln and Eva Stephenson

We have named our son my grandfather's first name—the grandfather where my last name came from.

—Stephanie Brill, mother of Charlie Thompson

My daughter has my nana's first name as her middle name.

—Jessica Worrall, mother of Elise Worrall

[We didn't pass on the] last name, but my dad's first name. It was more about honoring my parents than the name.

—Rebecca Stock, mother of Logan Galea

Inez was given Kosak as a middle name, as this was an old name in Ben's family that was discarded at the time of Ben's grandmother's remarriage.

—Daine Singer, mother of Inez Singer

If we have a boy, he will be Henry Hibbs (encompassing both last names, with one as a first name. Henry was also my great-uncle). If we have a girl, her first name will be linked to my side of the family (haven't worked out how, yet!)

—Eliza-Jane Henry-Jones, married

Or you might decide not to honor family at all ...

Someone made a suggestion that I called the baby Carter if it was a boy to honor [the name], but they didn't know I hated my last name at that point.

—Melissa Carter, mother of Finlay Inglis

We had a lot of conflict with my partner's parents because my mother-in-law, who is of Irish heritage, wanted us to use her maiden name in some way. This was because she was one of two girls, and the name had thus been not carried on. I was very resistant because I felt it unfair that the child should carry so much of them and so little of me. I figured, if the baby isn't having my last name, he's certainly not having someone else's, someone I have very little connection with. It caused quite a bit of tension.

—Jessie Cole, mother of Milla and Luca Finardi

I am not that fond of my last name. It would be unthinkable for me to change my name, but I'm glad to have my daughter and husband share a last name. I think it makes it easier for his family to understand me. They probably find it a bit unusual that I didn't take my husband's name.

—Sari Fordham, mother of Kai Bradford

Despite feeling strongly about keeping my own name, I never really questioned the use of my husband's name for the children. I don't really know why now, it seems weird. I also have some hang-ups about my own family unhappiness, and felt my husband's family were a more united and cohesive unit. Years later I realize they are mental like my family.

—Sarah McCallan, mother of Philippa and Benjamin Wallace

No [we didn't acknowledge my family in the last name choices]. However, in line with our traditions, both my children were bestowed with Yolngu names, and totems. (Yolngu people do not choose the names of their children. Names are bestowed by elders in the clan group. It is considered particularly auspicious if multiple people bestow names to your child. As a result, all Yolngu people have many names. Often, they have a public name, as well as one or two names that close family refer to them by).

—Mayatili Marika, mother of Thomas and Tessa Griffin

We talk about having another child and quite possibly that child will have [my husband's] last name. Another joke while pregnant was that Taylor [my husband's last name] would be the child's first name ... And then other jokesters said Taylor Taylor would be fun, like Courtney Taylor-Taylor, and all the funny friends were uninvited to all the things.

—Amelia Chappelow, mother of Felix Chappelow

FINAL WORDS ABOUT LAST NAMES

Now you've heard lots of stories of what other people have done. But the final decision of what last name you give your child is ultimately up to you. It's time to take the conversation out of the pages of this book and into the real world, and open up the discussion with your partner. Now that you are armed with six different options, I hope that together you can find a solution that feels right for you. Good luck!

I think you're giving your child an identity and a name they have to live with. If you don't like your own last name, then don't feel like you have to pass it on. Don't worry about whether you'll offend someone if you don't pass on tradition or cover both bases (such as using hyphens). Give your children a name they can feel proud telling someone or writing down on a form. Think about how it sounds together (Avery Yogi sounded silly) and do what works for you and your child.

—Renae Whale, mother of Avery Carolan

Whether you're in a same-sex or heterosexual relationship, I think it should be talked about thoroughly and there should not be room for regret. Nor do I think it should just be a rule that the last name of the father should be adopted.

—Cecilia Acevedo, mother of Silas Acevedo

I think we name children too quickly. Some people even find out the gender of their child and give them a first name before they are born. I wish last names could be decided a while after the child is born. My own daughter strongly represents her father's character, and if I had known how similar their personalities would be I think I would have pushed harder to use my last name.

—Megan Parker, mother of Iris O'Neill

Why do a majority of straight men get so touchy about the subject? Even really great, feminist, "enlightened" men I've known over the years seem to feel threatened if a last name option other than theirs is considered. They might deign to think about both names, but just the mother's name seems to be a no-go zone for them. Why? Patriarchal hangover? Do they think that it means that their paternity or their masculinity will be questioned if their children have a different name to them?

—Sarah Baker, mother of June Baker

I think that the decision of a child's last name has already become less of a given (that it will be the father's name) and more of a choice, like the first or middle name. I think with this will come more acceptance of people's different choices.

—Sophie Fernandes, mother of "Roo" Fernandes

Giving your child the father's last name won't make [the father] a more actively involved parent.

—Emily Goode, mother of Arlo, Bertrand and Lyle Godfrey

I think children should have both their mother and father's last name to begin with, and then change to what they prefer when they're adults.

—Joanna Peppas, mother of Jennifer Gray

In recent years I've thought about the bad stuff a name can bring. [There is so] much history, good and bad, in my last name. Lots of stories seem to repeat themselves in families, and we actually talked about whether or not changing a last name, or choosing not to give a particular one to a kid, might stop a particular dysfunctional recurring family story or cycle. [It's an interesting] idea anyway. I think names are important for all those reasons.

—Linda Roberts, mother of Lev and Zadie Roberts

I think in this day and age, there is much more acceptance about varying last names. I know two couples that have combined both their last names to honor each other. I also know one family who decided to give the mother's last name to their children, rather than the father's, so that they would be able to get into particular schools. It's great that the discussion can be had, and that people have more choice.

—Mayatili Marika, mother of Thomas and Tessa Griffin

Names matter: they carry identity that we invest. And certainly we can change them or disregard them or make them mean more—but it's something intensely personal that is external, and [a way] for all the world to see my children.

—Diane Tam, mother of Jude and Lou Tarricone-Tam

I only know one straight couple where the kids have their mother's last name. Seems ridiculous. Same-sex couples are more creative.

—Helen Ross, mother of Zoe Ross and Flynn Harding-Ross

I think too much emphasis is put on the right of males to assert their heirs through names. If a mother's last name is used it is often as a middle name or a hyphen.

I think women should feel completely empowered to choose their last name for their children without the father feeling rejected or upset. Men need to get over the need to claim ownership over their children's lives through names and feel connected by being a present parent instead.

—Elyse Truex, mother of Leon Truex

Personally I think the Icelandic system is the only one that makes sense. I would like to be able to trace my matrilineal heritage in that way.

—Clare Chippendale, mother of Ginger Rogers

I find it concerning that so many women still feel they cannot even challenge the idea that their children have only their husband's name. It clearly demonstrates that we still live in a patriarchal culture. Even though women are the ones with the powerful biology that produces and sustains life, we still pander to men in nearly every way, and it infuriates me!

—Kate Hegarty, mother of Theodore and Percival Hegarty-Bowen

It'd be best if we all just had given names, like Madonna.

—Samone Bos, mother of Saffron and Jasper Bos

I wish more families would think and choose rather than re-create a patriarchal lineage.

—Rachel Cowling, mother of Fergus and Evie Cowling

[The reason I] felt so certain that I wanted my daughter to have my name was not just the fact that I like my name, but also that I really dislike the patriarchal practice of babies taking their father's last name. I feel like our society should have progressed a little beyond this—at least to the point where there's a bit more of a mixed bag of last names. However, to me it still feels like the vast majority of kids still take their dad's name, and I think there are lots of women out there who would love for their children to have their last name but who buckle under societal pressure and end up conforming. I knew that I didn't want that to be me. (I know that a lot of women are perfectly happy to give up their name, and that is fine too, of course, I just want there to be a genuine choice for women.)

—Jane Winning, mother of Elva Ribush-Winning

I just love that our generation is able to have the conversation.

—Mary Masters, mother of Gideon Binstead

Any knuckle-dragger who does insist on their kids having their last name and won't compromise is not somebody you should be having kids with.

—Chris Dite, single

It's such a personal decision and I love the different variations and combinations that people choose.

—Ilana Jaffe, mother of Abe Hoffman

Women's lineage matters. It should be considered and included. Wives and children are their own people and having their own names is not a threat to the family unity. Partners should discuss names rather than just adhering to traditional naming conventions. Discussion and consideration is a great way to find a name that suits your family and is in line with your worldviews. It is also a great way to halt the continuation of truly cringeworthy family names like Bongers, Ballitch, and Rape.

—Cindy Renate, mother of Arminka Axelle and Elke Seraphine

I wish people would subject the name combination of given name and last name (for example: Ernest Gray McBurney) to the supermarket test before naming their child, including diminutives. This means simulating a supermarket situation, loudly: "Ernie McBurney, put that down this instant!"

—Lesley McBurney, mother of Heather and David McBurney

I love the trend of mashing names together as an alternative to hyphenation, and wish I could have done that elegantly. It's lovely to see all these possibilities emerging. I remember how much of a big deal it was at school for a friend's mother to have kept her own name, and that was only twenty years ago. Now few people even bat an eyelid.

—Jessica Friedmann, mother of Owen Baylis

They will have interesting decisions to make when they have children of their own!

—Jeanette Elliott, mother of Elizabeth, Miriam and Suzannah Elliott Haynes

I feel like baby last names are not really discussed by couples, it

*is just the default that the father's name will be used. Even when the mother has not changed their name, the father's name is used. I do not know anybody else who has used the mother's last name. It seems to be mass compliancy: why aren't more women wanting to pass on their family name? In our post–*Mad Men* age of (alleged) equality surely we should be seeing more than 3 per cent of couples using the mother's last name?!*

—Erin Jeffers, mother of Eva Jeffers

There is a lot of handwringing that is done by parents now because we're afforded the consideration of options that previous generations didn't have, but when our children grow up, they can change their names to whatever they choose to, as we can too (and some of us have done). Some of them will hate their ordinary-sounding names, some of them will feel the weight of their unusual ones, while others will settle into theirs without a second thought. In the end, parents can give their children whatever name they like, but they will have little control over how their children will grow up with them.

—Hop Dac Nguyen, father of Georgette Nguyen

I truly love the blended name thing. A friend of mine had the option (Watt and Mann becoming Wattmann) but didn't do it because of family pressure. I can't wait for the day when it's more common.

—Melinda Phelps, in a relationship

I've had a number of people ask me why I (1) didn't change my name when I got married and (2) didn't change it once I had a baby. It seems confounding to some people that I would willingly have a different name to my child. But, you know, it doesn't make us any less connected because we don't share the same last name. In saying that, it was important to me that Molly have Murphy appear somewhere in her full name ... so that I was represented, so to speak.

—Kathleen Murphy, mother of Molly Wardle

I can't wait to hear what creative solutions people have come up with. People are amazing sometimes and I can't wait to be inspired.

—Alister McCulloch, in a relationship

One lovely thing happened when Felix was three months old. We visited Hobart and saw an old work colleague of mine who had two kids ... And the six-year-old was so excited to meet our little Baby Felix ... She kept talking about Felix Huckleberry Chappelow and then it morphed into Felix Chuckleberry ... And now we call our family The Chuckleberrys ... I love it, so altogether we are some funny folksy farmer family ... And so begins our story together as a new family.

There is more to a name, and the newness we felt as parents, with our boy, we feel unique, we are all doing this together and running our own race ... So our family is like this, and your family is like yours.

—Amelia Chappelow, mother of Felix Chappelow

It's such a personal decision, and many of my friends have changed their names in marriage so they share their kids' names. I'm not sure why the fathers' last name is still the most common option amongst my (supposedly) liberated generation; it seems there has been a conservative swing towards patriarchal traditions. I feel lucky that I have a partner who is open to alternative names, and also lucky that our names sound good together!

—Clare Rae, mother of Fox Palmerae

I cannot believe women keep caving with bullshit excuses. It's disappointing and revealing.

—Catherine Deveny, mother of Dom, Hugo and Charlie Deveny-Borg

Having different last names caused administrative problems for my sister once her kids started going to childcare and school. I'm not sure whether this is a normal experience, or if those places were particularly shit. I'd be interested to know how the typical experience varies for people in different areas, but that's just my curiosity. Surely this kind of thing is becoming more common so you'd think stuff like IT systems not coping would start to be addressed?

—Alex Maher, in a relationship

This is for me the clearest, most empirically demonstrable example of social pressures. Everyone claims to have a free choice, yet 90 per cent go in one direction. Both cannot be true and the statistics are hard to refute.

—Martin Bush, father of Remi and Aida Oke

I think it's nice for people to give their kids whatever last name they please.

—Eileen Kenny, in a relationship

In the same way I don't like the practice of women blindly taking on their partner's last names, I don't like the idea of children automatically being named after their fathers. Whatever they end up being named should be very carefully considered and discussed, and not a given.

—Eliza-Jane Henry-Jones, married

At this point I'm not sure it really matters but maybe I'd feel differently once I have a child. Naming a pet is pretty hard so I guess choosing a baby last name would be quite hard. My dog has ended up with my partner's last name when we changed vet clinic and she was the first person to take him there—I feel quite strongly that the dog should have my last name, as I was the original owner before I met her.

—Ledger McDavitt, in a relationship

It's vexing! I wish we had an automatic system that combined last names or something and was thus fair and loved by all. Can you organize this?

—Sam Cooney, in a relationship

My personal ideal last name scenario is for my partner, myself and our children to all adopt my maternal great-grandmother's last name, as a compromise between maintaining a unified family name, upholding feminist values (with which only the wife changing her last name is inconsistent) and preserving *family history. I otherwise intend to use that name as a <u>middle</u> name for either a son or daughter.*

—Jane Greenbank, single

It's just so weird that people feel so strongly on the subject in this day and age. I kinda get that if you have some kind of noble family name you might want to preserve that (as gross as hereditary titles are), but the vast majority of family names in the contemporary West mean absolutely nothing. (At least for white people—I can imagine that it's very different for people with non-Anglo last names, and that keeping such last names might be an act of resistance against a white cultural hegemony.)

—Chad Parkhill, married

I know this is probably a shallow statement but I want my children to have beautiful sounding names. I want people to repeat them out loud when they meet because it sounds so harmonious to the ear. I want my children to be incredible, interesting, kind people who have interesting, incredible names that resonate.

—Agatha Morse, married

I think all babies should officially be called Baby Babybabybaby until the age of two.

—Alex Campbell, in a relationship

I wish people would make a range of choices. My friends are feminists, yet somehow their children always end up with the father's last name. That's their right to choose, obviously, but there are options and no one way is right. I can appreciate that for a lot of people there are both family pressures and worries over cumbersome combinations.

—David Laurence, in a relationship

Fuck patrilineal traditions! Girls deserve to have their own names. Mothers deserve their names to be remembered.

—Jessica Alice, in a relationship

So many women (and men) that I know agree "in theory" that it should be a negotiation and not just a given which last name is used. However, I reckon that for every five women I know who have said the couple is open to using either last name, four of them go with the father's name, because it still is seen as the path of least resistance, and there's always some other "excuse" for it even though "we considered using my name". Not a judg-

ment, just an observation, and I can see myself falling into that category too.

—Ellie Higgins, in a relationship

Call me old-fashioned but I do like the notion of a last name carrying forward, albeit a hyphenated composite. I believe in an innate desire for most to be inquisitive about their roots and fore bearers. That said, however, I have no issue whatsoever in establishing a new name and lineage. As in life in general— each to their own.

—Kurt Luthy, single

I wish I'd been brave enough to create a new last name. It would have been cool.

—Sarah McCallan, mother of Philippa and Benjamin Wallace

People often talk about how this is a choice parents and families all have to make for themselves and we shouldn't judge and it's all up to the individual and blah blah blah. I think that is bullshit. If it was really a free choice, as many men would give up their last name at marriage as women do. As many children would have their mother's last name as their father's. No one is making free choices here, there are no free choices. And women owe it to themselves and their children to force the issue and not give up their names and naming rights over children so easily. Women have been loving children regardless of their names since time immemorial; surely men can learn to do the same. Any man who feels weird about having children with a different last name to himself is too immature to be having children in the first place.

—Zora Sanders, married

As far as I can see, a last name performs three basic functions. It provides an identification with one's ancestry—letting you see yourself as a continuation of a line. It gives a sense of common identity with one's parents and siblings. And it gives another sense of common identity with one's children and, perhaps, partner, should they adopt it. Last names are triple-jobbing with inevitable impacts on their performance. The system we generally use requires the abandonment of the mother's maiden name in order to continue functioning. An ugly work-around that is unfair (which bothers me) as well as being inefficient and messy (which bothers me considerably more). One common attempt to solve the issue is double-barreling, but this isn't so much a solution as a short-termist hack that passes the problem onto the next generation. A complete overhaul is needed. I suggest the following:

Boys take their father's last name, girls take their mother's last name. Simple. Function 1 (lineage) is served. Functions 2 and 3 are not.

Abandon traditional middle names. This space can be put to more meaningful use. A family name. A name shared only with one's parents and siblings. A label for this and only this family grouping. This name is selected by the parents upon their marriage or the birth of their first child. Function 2 is served.

If and when the child themselves attains adulthood and takes a partner, they in turn choose another name. A name they can share with each other and their own offspring.

And of course everyone must have their own individual given name, as is the case now. The pattern end up as follows:

<Given name> <Name shared with parents and siblings> <Name shared with partner and children> <Name shared with gender-specific ancestry>

Four names in total doesn't seem unreasonable to manage. In fact, more can be added should someone have multiple families. Half-siblings present no problem to the system. Everyone's name could consist of a series of terms, each one of each binds them to a family. No identifiers need ever be sacrificed so no information need be lost.

—Myles Cuffe, father of Senan, Leonore and Luan Cuffe

Naming is one of those practices so fundamental to our beings that we tend to see it as being largely without political value. But I've always been very uncomfortable with the abnegation of identity implicit in surrendering one's name, both in marriage and childbirth. Of course it's a choice and few women in this era would profess to being forced into it, but on a prac-

tical level it strikes me as objectively insane that fathers get naming priority at all, given how partially involved we are with the process. But who knows? Perhaps when push comes to shove and idle theorizing comes to imminent parenthood some deep spark of identity preservation will well up and push my stake to the fore. I hope not, but from observation having a kid seems to make short work of one's loftier ideals.

—Luke Ryan, married

ABOUT THE AUTHOR

Lorelei Vashti is an Australian writer and editor. Her first book *Dress, Memory: A Memoir of My Twenties in Dresses*, was based on her popular blog dressmemory.com.

She lives with her partner and two children, and runs Jacky Winter Gardens, a guesthouse and artist in residence program in Victoria's Dandenong Ranges.

She has contributed to numerous anthologies including *Mothermorphosis*, *Australia's Best Comedy Writing*, and the *Women of Letters* series, and is currently working on her first play.

instagram.com/loreleivashti

www.ingramcontent.com/pod-product-compliance
Lightning Source LLC
Chambersburg PA
CBHW020318010526
44107CB00054B/1885